Published by:
Read Communications, a division of MRG, Inc.
1372 Old Stage Rd
Williston, Vermont 05495 USA
www.MRgrp-us.com

Designed by: Averiel Hossley

Library of Congress Cataloging-in-Publication Data

Read, Markey
Launch, Grow & Prosper as a Woman Solopreneur
ISBN-0-9636685-7-9

Launch, Grow, & Prosper

as a Woman Solopreneur

by Markey Read

Table of Contents

Foreword

As the founder and CEO of eWomenNetwork, I've had the privilege of witnessing countless journeys of entrepreneurial spirit, determination, and success. It is within this vibrant community of driven women entrepreneurs that I've come to know and respect Markey Read, whose depth of insight, breadth of knowledge, and unwavering commitment to supporting individuals in crafting businesses that not only succeed but prosper like never before, are truly commendable. Markey stands out not just for her solid foundation and 30+ years as a business owner, but also for her approach to client engagement—marked by a healthy dose of optimism and an invaluable sense of humor.

Markey offers both practical advice and inspirational guidance, as she peels back the curtain to share the lessons of her journey as a business owner. She does this all with humility and heartfelt honesty that lets us know she is committed to lifting others as she climbs. Her personal narratives of heartbreak and triumph resonate deeply, serving as a beacon for those navigating the often-tumultuous waters of entrepreneurship. "Launch, Grow, and Prosper as a Woman Solopreneur" is more than a book; it's a testament to Markey's dedication to helping others create businesses that are not only unique to their vision but also aligned with the rewards they aim to gain by departing from conventional employment.

This book is crucial, especially in today's fast-paced, ever-evolving business landscape. Markey addresses the pressing challenges and opportunities facing women Solopreneurs with precision and empathy. From honing an entrepreneurial mindset and leveraging natural talents to defining services, understanding customers, and crafting effective marketing strategies, this book covers the essential components of building a scalable and sustainable business.

For readers delving into this treasure trove of wisdom, know that you are embarking on a journey to elevate your professional and personal expertise into a viable and prosperous business. The book guides you through the nuances of pricing, client segmentation, networking, and creating a marketing strategy that resonates with your unique selling proposition. Additionally, it will help you navigate the critical aspects of sales pipelines, negotiations, ti me and energy management, and ultimately, the ability to set yourself up for success by understanding your natural personality style and the critical importance of building a supportive team.

Why should you, the reader, care about this book's subject matter? Because at its core, "Launch, Grow, and Prosper" is about transformation—your transformation. It is a guide designed to help you, especially if you are a woman Solopreneur at the crossroads of transitioning to a CEO, to navigate the complexities of growth, leadership, and personal fulfillment. This book is not just about building a business; it's about building a life that you love, filled with the balance, growth, and success you deserve.

Markey Read's "Launch, Grow, and Prosper as a Woman Solopreneur" is a beacon for those ready to make a significant impact through their business. It's an invitation to embark on a journey of growth, leadership, and prosperity. With Markey's guidance, you're not just launching a business; you're launching a future of possibilities.

Sandra Yancey,
Founder & CEO eWomenNetwork

Welcome!

Being in business for yourself is one of the most powerful journeys of self-discovery and self-mastery available today. It's an opportunity to bring your brilliance into the world and make a lasting and meaningful difference in other people's lives.

Your journey from idea to marketplace will be full of challenges, opportunities, amazing moments, setbacks, and breakthroughs. There are days it will be easy as pie and others when it will seem monumentally difficult. If you stay focused on why you do what you do, you will be compelled into a future unlike your past and receive rewards beyond your imagination.

I have been an enterprising and entrepreneurial woman for as long as I can remember and have started and abandoned several businesses since I was a teenager. What I learned in one endeavor magically prepared me for the next and encouraged me to stay on my path as an entrepreneur until I found the kind of business that truly resonated with me.

> *I encourage you to get clear about your Superpowers and your Bozopowers, stand tall in your strengths and develop a sense of humor about your less developed abilities.*

In 1992 I transitioned from contractor to business partner in the business that I eventually came to own as a sole owner. I have made just about every mistake possible and lived to tell my story today. I have experienced remarkable success because of a combination of implacable momentum, strategic planning, daily devotion, and an extensive network of generous and helpful people. In this book I share many of these stories to help you find your footing, forge your path, and achieve your successes.

Throughout this process, I encourage you to get clear about your Superpowers and your Bozopowers, stand tall in your strengths and develop a sense of humor about your less developed abilities. Knowing which jobs and tasks are yours to do and which are not will give you the focus needed to build your dream. These distinctions are essential to creating a prosperous business. Business can be hard, but it doesn't have to be impossibly hard.

When I sat down to write this book in 2020, I wanted to write the entrepreneurial guide to end all guides, but I would still be writing that book if I included everything I know about being in business. The lessons, insights, and knowledge in this book are foundational. Know that there is much more to building a business than what is included here, but having a solid base will enable you to build a business that you love.

How to Use this Book:

If you have been in business for a while, use this book to fill in the gaps. If pricing is still confounding, start in Chapter 3: **How Do I Make a Living**? If you want to develop a referral network, turn to Chapter 6: **How Can I Network Like a Pro?** If you are not sure who your primary, secondary, and tertiary customers are, use Chapter 2: **What are you Selling & Who is Buying?** to get clear about your best fit customer. Wherever you are on your journey, you will find practical and inspirational resources and stories for support in getting to the next level.

If you are just starting or are in the first couple of years of your business, use the progression of the book as a guide to your adventure. In the first chapter, you have a quick reference guide to getting clear about your concept and setting yourself up for success. Each subsequent chapter will help you delve deeper into identifying your best-fit clients, developing fabulous services, establishing a dynamic pricing strategy, and marketing your services.

> *Launch, Grow and Proster as a Woman Solopreneur is a treasure map. Let this book be your guide to creating a business you love and that loves you in return.*

Launch, Grow & Prosper as a Woman Solopreneur is a treasure map. Let this book be your guide to creating a business you love and that loves you in return. There is an abundance of riches ahead!

Each chapter answers an essential question
Are you a Solopreneur?
What are you selling?
Who is buying?
How to I make a living?
How can I refine my pricing?
How will I get the word out?
How can I network like a pro?
How do I create a marketing strategy?
How do I fill my pipeline & close the deal?
How do I manage my time and energy?
How do I set myself up for success?

We'll start with are you a Solopreneur? This first leg of the journey will help you navigate through understanding your entrepreneurial mindset and motivations. This process is deeply personal, tapping into your skills, talents, and the vision you hold for the future. It's about identifying your Superpowers, the unique attributes that set you apart, and connecting with those who need what you have to offer—your ideal clients.

Next, we'll delve into *what you're selling and who is buying.* Defining your services is just the beginning. We'll explore your target audience, size up the competition, and clarify your Unique Selling Proposition (USP). With these insights, we create a business roadmap tailored just for you, guiding your journey with precision and purpose.

The most pressing issue every entrepreneur must address is *how to make a living.* This is where we tackle the essentials of pricing your services. From setting your base prices with smart, adaptable strategies to managing fees and exploring ways to enhance your income. We cover it all. It's about finding the right balance that rewards your expertise while providing value to your clients.

When it's time to further refine your pricing, we'll take a closer look at your offerings and the clients you serve. Through a deeper understanding of market segmentation, we refine where to direct your marketing efforts, ensuring optimization.

Once you have the basics in place, you will learn *how to get the word out.* Crafting a compelling marketing and promotional plan is crucial. We revisit your USP and develop a branding story that captures the essence of what you offer, ensuring your message reaches the right ears and hearts.

People buy from people they know, like, and trust; networking is a powerful method to solidify the necessary connections. Whether it's connecting in one-on-one engagements, engaging in small group interactions, or making an impact at a large event, you will learn to network like a pro and expand your business through meaningful connections and a solid referral network.

In *how to create a marketing strategy,* we distinguish between the various facets of marketing—advertising, public relations, personal selling, and more—to build a comprehensive strategy that leverages your key value propositions and maximizes return on investment.

No matter how amazing your services are, you still need to fill your pipeline and close the deal. Here we'll explore strategies for maintaining a robust sales pipeline, negotiating confidently, and standing firm in your value during those pivotal moments.

Because each of us only has 24 hours in a day, *learning how to manage your time and energy* will help you balance the demands of business with personal well-being. This is an artform and this section offers guidance on setting boundaries, managing expectations, and ensuring that your entrepreneurial journey enhances your life, not complicates it.

And finally, it's important to set *yourself up for success.* Discovering your natural personality style and leveraging your inherent strengths lays the foundation for success. We'll also touch on the basics of corporate structures and building your team to support your growth.

May your journey be filled with remarkable celebrations, opportunities to gain experience, insights, and inspirations about how to serve your clients, and mostly may it be Fabulous!

1
Are You a Solopreneur?

The Stories We Tell Ourselves

People are so creative! They tell themselves the most amazing stories about why they cannot start a business. These stories range in genre from romantic fantasy to blood-curdling horror. The a few popular refrains are:

I have to have enough savings to live for three years before starting.

I have to make a choice between my family or my choice to start a business.

I have to have the perfect website or logo or marketing campaign before launching.

I have to get an MBA or Certification to be qualified for what I want to do.

For Solopreneurs who provide professional services, including training, coaching, advising, consulting, none of these story lines are useful or true. It's time to tell a different story!

I Have to Have Enough Savings to Live for Three Years Before Starting

If you talk to the Small Business Administration or bankers or other traditional sources of business start-up resources, most will stand by this standard piece of advice because they are used to serving a certain sector of business. This generic concept assumes you have equipment, inventory, raw materials, office or manufacturing space, staff, and other fixed start-up costs. These are typical costs for a manufacturing business. It also assumes a significant lag between launching your business and generating income.

Most service-focused Solopreneurs I work with need to buy a computer, relevant software, a good printer, and a few office supplies. If you already have a laptop computer with some basic software, it makes sense to start using what you have already and build from there. Over time you will buy a better computer, invest in a higher quality printer, update your software, and figure out which supplies you really need to keep on hand.

Regarding income generation, it's much easier for a service provider to pick up projects and contracts to generate fast cash than it is for a manufacturer. In fact, most consultants start with a project here and there on the side of a full-time job or as a way to fill the gap between jobs. For many, the potential for generating their income by growing their consulting practice compared to getting a full-time job again is enough for them to take their destiny into their own hands and become Solopreneurs.

Remember: any paper, printer ink, and/or other supplies you use to produce materials should be folded into your fees and charged to your client.

You may not generate all the income you need in the first year, but if you have been actively developing your referral network, it will come. In the first few years you will attract customers that are not exactly your ideal and will likely accept projects that are not absolutely core to your vision. While I am a great believer in sticking to ideals, I recommend that you gladly take these slightly off-center projects to generate income and create some financial stability. You will attract the clients and projects that you CAN do, and these will lead to the projects you WANT to do. The exceptions are illegal activities, jobs that are against your personal morals or values, or that cost you more to fulfill than you will generate.

Throughout my first year in business, I had a part-time job. I needed a regular paycheck that paid my basic bills and some non-traditional hours that allowed me to see clients during the day. I took that job knowing it was temporary, a means to an end. I worked all kinds of weird hours between my part-time job and client appointments but exactly a year later, I quit the job and stepped into being a full-time consultant and coach.

I Have to Make a Choice Between My Family or My New Business

The short answer is "no, you don't."

This concept is based on a narrowly defined model of success that demands a 24/7 focus on the business while sacrificing everything else.

Yes, you will probably think about your business all the time, but you probably think about your job for more hours than you are physically present, too. As a Solopreneur, instead of thinking about how to make someone else money, you can focus on growing your own income.

The real difference, however, is what is defined as working "on" your business. The generally accepted standard for consultants is 20 hours of billable time per week. The rest of the time, you will be marketing, networking, creating new materials, filing, entering your receipts, and whatever else you need to do to keep the piles on your desk at bay and the clients coming in. You are free to work more hours and bill more time, but if you are billing 30+ a week and barely scraping by financially, it's time to raise your rates and reduce your billable hours. Base your hourly rate on the assumption that you will bill 20 hours a week and generate the income you need to pay yourself, pay your bills, and invest in your business

I Have to Have the Perfect Website or Logo or Marketing Campaign Before Launching

This is just straight up procrastination! You will never have a perfect website or logo or marketing campaign. This is an impossible ideal and just keeps you spinning in place. Even if you could get close to perfect, as soon as you start your work, something will change; then change again in a year and continue to change for the rest of time.

The first steps for a consultant are to figure out the basic services to offer and the people you think will be interested in buying those services. Then get yourself in front of the

people who will make the decision to buy what you are selling and demonstrate your brilliance. The most amazing website or logo is not what sells consulting, coaching, or other professional services. You are what sells your services.

My first logo was just the name of my business in a font that appealed to me; I've had a website since the beginning of time. However neither us the reason I've been hired. People hire people. Your clients are buying you, your knowledge, your experience, your approach, your Superpowers. Engage with your target market and they will engage you.

I Have to Get an MBA or Certification

This one naturally follows from the needs for a perfect website and marketing campaign. It is a dressed-up version of Imposter Syndrome. If you think you need an objective measure of your competence before launching, you are being too hard on yourself. When you accurately demonstrate your level of knowledge, expertise, and experience, there will always be someone who needs your level of expertise. Your ideal clients may be executives in large organizations, but you can start with emerging leaders and build your reputation. You may want to be a keynote speaker at international conferences, but you can start by speaking to local organizations and conferences to build your following. Over time, you may want to add a degree or certification to your credentials, but you don't need one to get started.

I never held an executive level position until I was president of my own company. My undergraduate degree was English, and my first career was journalism. My degree and work history were not necessarily my strengths. Being a journalist was.

As a journalist, I became adept in quickly absorbing new information, asking good questions, listening carefully, taking lots of notes, and assimilating all that into a coherent article within tight deadlines. I let new corporate clients talk and they revealed the darndest things. I started hearing their pain points, gaps, and opportunities. I built on those skills when I returned to my office: I did some research, picked the brains of a few colleagues, used other people's materials (with permission of course), and put together some fairly good programs for my first few corporate clients.

Looking back on those programs, I confess I am a little embarrassed. But one of my coaches often says that if you are not embarrassed by your early work, you waited too long to start.

No Two Businesses are Alike

Remember that there is no right way to do business. Averages, norms, and standards are just theoretical concepts and do not exist in nature. Did you know that every single apple seed produces a completely different variety of apple? The only way to guarantee that a new Honey Crisp apple tree will produce a true Honey Crisp apple is to literally cut a branch off the parent tree and graft it onto a new root stock. It's called cloning. You are not a clone and neither is your business. Define your business on your terms.

Shifting from Employee to Entrepreneur

What Is Your Entrepreneurial Mindset?

To shift from being an employee to an entrepreneur requires a shift in thinking. If you don't see yourself as enterprising, it may be helpful to review your origin story.

Let's start this process by taking a look at your beliefs about being a Solopreneur. In my experience, our beliefs or mindset are vitally important to our ability to launch, grow, and prosper as Solopreneurs. These beliefs influence our entrepreneurial origin story.

The people around you help shape your mythos. These people may be family members or friends. Reflecting on our stories can give us important clues about our own entrepreneurial journeys. If you grew up thinking entrepreneurs are dreamers or workaholics for example, you need another point of reference to fully embrace the entrepreneurial life.

The biggest players in my story were various characters from my family of origin. My family is filled with stories of entrepreneurial and enterprising folks. For example, I am the great granddaughter of the people who started what is now known as ConAgra, one of the largest food conglomerates in the world. My mother's father's family hail from Nebraska and in the 1890's they bought a defunct grain mill along the Platt River; they rebuilt it stone by stone and started milling grain for their neighbors. Eventually, they partnered with two other mills along the Platt, becoming Consolidated Mills of Nebraska and then ConAgra. As fiscally conservative midwesterners, they managed to stay alive through the Depression and then methodically built a thriving enterprise. I grew up with the belief that if you worked hard and stayed committed you could create something important and lasting.

On my father's side, I have a completely different heritage. The most memorable stories I heard are all about my aunt. She is a serial entrepreneur and has gone through multiple boom and bust cycles as she has journeyed through various businesses including a casino in Montana that literally went up in flames. The stories about her are filled with humor, horror, and resiliency. She always landed on her feet. Through her adventures, I learned that, even when it looks as if you failed, you can always start anew.

These two stories provided me with a fantastic range of what is possible as an entrepreneur. Both stories involved taking risks. Both stories have great successes and great losses. The two big lessons I heard in these legendary tales are that you can start small or big but, however you start, build a business that suits you.

If you have already started and stopped a business or two, for whatever reason, you may not have found the right fit. All types of people are capable of starting and building a business, but not all businesses are for all types of people.

I started and stopped two businesses before becoming a partner in the business I eventually came to own. After being constantly frustrated as an employee and getting myself fired a few times in the process, I decided to write a new story where the heroine is a successful entrepreneur.

Take a moment now to think about the stories that inform your beliefs about being in business for yourself. Look for people who took risks, stood outside the cultural norms, and created something from nothing. They may not have been wildly successful or moved through many cycles of bust and boom. What's key is that they made an impression on you.

Who were family members, friends of the family, neighbors that were entrepreneurs? What messages did you get about them when family members or friends recounted their stories? Were those people seen as irresponsible, brilliant but misguided or as innovative geniuses, hardworking and honest?

Getting Clear About Your Why

What Are Your Motivations?

Now let's take a look at your motivation for being in business. This is about finding your why or your core motivations. Yes, making an income is part of this, but I want you to dig a little deeper.

Owning your own business is a powerful way to express your professional talents and expertise. It can also be one of the most challenging journeys you undertake. So, it's time to get really clear with yourself about your "why."

There are other ways to make a living, many of which are easier and provide more stability. So, you need to really think about why you want to enter into this realm. While it's important that you have a clear vision, mission, and purpose, it's also important that your business fits your personal and professional aspirations.

Operating a business that's in conflict with your personal needs or values, or a business that lacks the potential to provide you with the opportunity to meet your professional goals, will just be a lot of bother without much reward.

I wanted to be in business for myself since my mid-20s. I was dissatisfied with working for other people and figured if I was going to work so hard, why not build something that would build a future for me? When I did a quick inventory of my skills, I decided to start a business based on my sewing skills. I had been making my own clothes for years and I figured I could have a more flexible lifestyle and pay the rent if I made clothing for other people. After about a year, I came to the realization that I'm not a particularly good seamstress. Yes, I knew how to knock out a dress for myself in short order, but I never cared what the inside seams looked like. Additionally, I found out that I don't like sewing for other people and could never charge people for the number of hours I spent making their blouses and skirts. It turns out that working to pay the rent wasn't enough of a motivation for me. Sewing felt practical, but it never excited me enough to overcome the challenges.

When I connected to my core motivations - helping people live more fulfilling lives - I was able to use skills and talents I had already developed as a journalist and apply them to helping people represent themselves more clearly so they could get better jobs.

Once I realized people would pay me for this and pay me a lot more than they would for making their clothes, I never looked back.

You may have a big idea or vision that motivates you; or feel like you are on a mission of some kind; or even feel a sense of purpose about using your natural gifts. These are all good places to start. The good news is that you don't have to have it all figured out before you start and you can add, delete, and reroute once you have launched. Taking some time, however, to answer a few fundamental questions before launching will help you start your journey with a stronger sense of why you are bothering.

What are your motivations? Why do you want to be in business for yourself? What does being a Solopreneur symbolize or mean to you?

Starting With What You Have

What Are Your Skills, Talents, & Qualifications?

Being in business for yourself will require you to call on many different kinds of skills and talents. Most people base their businesses on their current skills and interests. Remember when I mentioned inventorying my skills before launching my sewing business? That's because it is a really good way to understand what you are starting with and what you may need to develop.

Skills alone, however, are a strong enough foundation from which to launch. I am a skilled seamstress, but not a talented one. I have been making my own clothes since I was 10 years old. I also grew up with a mother who was a puppet maker and spent many weekends selling her products at craft fairs. Sewing was familiar to me. In the end, however, it was too isolating. I need much more human interaction than I could get from sewing. Sew Fine didn't tap into my talents or serve my personality.

After closing up shop, I needed a job. My first career was in journalism, and I wanted to return to writing. When I tried getting a job with a magazine or publisher, I found that I didn't have the talents they were seeking. Eventually, I was hired as the distribution manager for a small publishing company that created and distributed a directory for steam passenger trains throughout North America.

In retrospect, it's no mystery why I was fired about six months later. I knew nothing about trains and was not really interested in learning about them. I did know databases and was organized, but I hated my job and it showed.

More convinced than ever that I wanted to be in business for myself, I made another attempt. I was interested in hospitality and fantasized about one day operating a bed and breakfast in the hills of Vermont. I wasn't in a position to start one and most places couldn't afford to hire me, so I looked for another way in. I wanted to understand the business so that when I was ready, I could launch my own bed and breakfast.

I decided to research and write a guide for bed & breakfasts in Vermont. After conducting a limited competition analysis, I discovered there was no directory of all the B&Bs in the state, so I launched Read Communications, and published *Vermont's Most Complete Book of Bed & Breakfasts*.

This was all before the ease of desktop publishing! While I was good at selling the idea to B&B owners, collecting the information, and distributing the book, I really did not like it. I quickly fell out of love with the hospitality industry. Again, I found most of the work associated with compiling and selling the book tedious. After the second edition, I literally closed the book on my fantasy of owning a B&B.

Technically, Read Communications didn't die with the book. I still publish under that name, but the only remnant of the book is the few copies of the second edition that I keep on my bookshelf to show people the first book I published.

Both of these businesses tapped into skills and interests; in the end they didn't keep my interest because they didn't employ my real talents or suit my personality. If you don't know what your talents are or what will suit your personality, take some time to understand yourself.

Skills, Talents & Qualifications

Since the word "skills" covers a lot of territory, let's look at three categories that may help you develop your inventory.

Skills are things we know how to do, but may not really enjoy. They could be innate or learned. I learned to sew as a young girl because my mother was a sewer and I figured out that she would buy fabric more readily than she would buy ready-made clothing. I liked clothes, so I learned to sew. I still make things using fabric but I don't want to sell those skills anymore.

Talents are innate gifts. We are often blind to them because they come naturally and we are usually surprised to discover that other people don't have the same level of ease. Listening to people's stories and helping them reframe them is a talent of mine. It's what made me a good journalist. I could quickly assimilate a lot of information and produce a coherent story.

Qualifications are earned. You may have a degree, certification, training, or years of experience in a field. When I started, I had very few qualifications. Now I have 30 years of experience, am certified in Emotional Intelligence (EQ), the Myers Briggs Type Indicator (MBTI), Positive Intelligence (PQ) and I have a Master's in Leadership and Group Dynamics.

Depending on how many years you have been on the planet, you may rely more on your talents or qualifications to start. Your skills will be useful, but I don't recommend leading with them as you develop your business.

As you write your inventory, don't make a fuss about distinguishing between skills, talents, and qualifications. Start with whatever comes to mind and write until you can't think of anything else. Take a break and when more ideas start flowing, add them to the list. Be sure to include any education, certifications, licensures, or other specialized training you have in your bag of tricks.

Accessing Your Superpowers

Where Do You Naturally Excel?

Just as all skills are not equal, neither are all talents. An overlooked subset of talents is your Superpowers. I didn't understand why people complimented me on my ability to command the attention of a room, for example. I thought everyone could do that. It turns out that not everyone can. Like talents, Superpowers are innate and usually invisible to us, but they reign supreme.

Superpowers are not completely unique to us, but combined with our personal experiences, they are what makes us distinct among all the other Superheroes out there.

Being in business for yourself is a lot like being a Superhero, but that does not mean you have to have the same Superpowers as all the other entrepreneurs. Identifying your unique powers is key to building a company that you can launch and grow.

Diana Prince (aka Wonder Woman) is one of my favorite Superheroes. Her many skills include those developed as she became an excellent horsewoman and archer: she can run and jump with the best of them! Among her people, the Amazons, these are commonplace skills. Among mere mortals, she stands out as incredibly talented.

Like our other talents, however, Superpowers can be hard to name. Remember, for Diana's Amazon sisters, it is banal to be an accomplished horsewoman and archer. It's only after she leaves her island and joins the Justice League that being the immortal daughter of Hippolyta and Zeus becomes her true Superpower, thus making her unique among all Superheroes. Because of her immense knowledge and exceptional perceptiveness, Diana Prince is the wisest and most emotionally intelligent member of the Justice League.

Swimming in the ocean of ourself, we can live for years without recognizing our Superpowers. I remember being in awe of other people's ability to lead groups and workshops in fun and engaging ways. I had a great desire to teach and lead groups but didn't think I had the abilities. While sitting next to a friend in a 2-day Myers-Briggs workshop, my friend spontaneously leaned over and said, "You could be doing that."

"Really?" I said in shock.

"Really," she said looking me dead in the eyes.

Within a few years, I was teaching engaging workshops, using the MBTI. Until she suggested it, I didn't see it for myself. The talents we admire in others are often qualities we possess but have not yet fully recognized.

Who are some of the people you admire? What qualities do they have that you think help them be successful?

If you were to interview them, what questions would you ask them about their "secret to success"? If the idea of identifying your Superpowers seems mystical to you, you may want to learn more about your Personality Type, or MBTI type. Knowing your Personality Type can provide insight into your talents and Superpowers.

What Stresses You Out is a Clue to your Personality Type

Use this quick reference chart to understand your Personality Type preferences. The suggestions included here are just suggestions, not rules.
(preferences = what you do 51% of the time)

Are you Stressed by:

Spending too much time alone and/or not having enough external stimulation	or	Spending too much time with others and/or having too many external distractions?

If you are stressed by too much time alone and/or not having enough stimulation, create a business that allows for plenty of interaction with others.	or	If you are stressed by spending too much time with others and/or too many external distractions, create a business that allows you to focus on smaller groups and individuals.

Are you Stressed by:

Living in ambiguity with no clear directions and ideas/concepts that lack any foundation or purpose	or	Having to follow exact detailed instructions and people who focus on the details before big picture?

If you are stressed by lack of clarity and broad concepts, create a business that focuses on concrete results.	or	If you are stressed by detailed instructions and data focused people, create a business that applies theory.

Are you Stressed by:

Decisions that seem illogical and subjective and being forced to worry about people rather than focus on the task	or	Not having your values respected in decision making and being in the midst of conflict and disharmony?

If you are stressed by a lack of logical decision making and being forced to focus on how people interact, serve a population whose focus is using well-founded tools and theories.	or	If you are stressed by a lack of values based decisions or disharmonious environments, serve a population whose focus is on getting along with others.

Are you Stressed by:

People and organizations that seem disorganized and rushing to finish at the last minute?	or	People and organizations that seem inflexible and being rushed into making decisions?

If you are stressed by seeming disorganization, create operating systems and schedules that give you the time you need to prepare and respond to clients	or	If you are stressed by seemingly rigid people and environments, create work environment that allows for a creative use of time.

Adapted from The eight core characters by OPP, © 2016

Bringing Benefit

What Difference Do You Want To Make?

Uniting your skills, talents, and qualifications with your motivations will lead you to the next step – determining what difference you want to make with your future clients.

Your talents, Superpowers, and qualifications provide valuable clues about the services you may consider offering; they are the building blocks of your services. You may be a naturally talented facilitator or have earned a qualification through education, training, or licensure. You may have a background in management, be a certified coach or project manager, or have a graduate-level degree in business or policymaking. These are all elements that will eventually define your services.

Beyond all your personal virtues, however, your clients will want to know what difference you will make -- that is to say, what kind of benefits or results you can produce as a talented facilitator or certified coach. They will wonder how your project management skills are a better fit for their needs than those of another consultant.

Writing, for example, is one of my Superpowers, but I don't want to write technical manuals or ghost write books. I want to use my abilities with language to help people lead better lives. Writing is the basis of much of what I offer, but the difference I make is that I help people get clear about who they are. I help them get on with being their wonderful selves.

Do you want to address the power dynamics between managers and their employees? Do you want to transform your industry to meet future challenges? Maybe you see yourself supporting emerging leaders or helping people become more competent in a technical arena. This goes beyond listing possible services; this is articulating the benefits your services will bring to your clients. How will their lives, teams, business, or boards be improved as a result of hiring you and your set of talents and qualifications?

If you are struggling with this, look back at your motivations for wanting to be in business in the first place. Beyond wanting to work for yourself or build your own empire, you are likely motivated to make a difference in some way.

In the beginning, I wanted to help professionals represent themselves better so they could get better jobs and improve their lives. This led me to creating resume , job search, and career planning services. Over time, the benefits of these services led me to create a 350-page workbook to support my clients through the process of growth, get more training and certifications in various tools, and teach people how to launch, grow, and prosper as entrepreneurs.

The benefits you will present may not be so clear in the beginning, so start by listing some services that you are thinking about offering. From there, think about what difference those services will make to the people who use them.

Writing resumes is a service; helping people tell their story so they are hired for jobs that are a better fit for them is a result, or benefit. What difference will your services make in the lives of your clients?

Finding Your People

Who Are Yours?

Simply put, your people are your first clients and customers. They are naturally attracted to your services, need your solutions, and see you as the person to resolve their challenges.

If you thought that everyone is your customer, by the way, think again. While you may be a lovely being offering incredible services, not everyone needs the kind of results you want to produce - at least not all at the same time.

You may want to serve private individuals, business owners, or executives. The kinds of benefits you provide will be a key indicator. When I started offering job search coaching and career counseling, for example, I wanted to serve professionals who were seeking better jobs and careers. This meant that my first customers were primarily college educated adults.

So instead of marketing to anyone and everyone, I focused on a subset of the general population: adults with college degrees seeking professional positions.

You may want to start by stating who you don't want to serve as a way to back into your customer description. For example, I instinctively knew that teens and college-age students were not my people. This is partly because I don't relate to them as well as I do with adults, but mostly because the kinds of benefits I wanted to provide are not a priority for people that are young. Until folks have been on the planet for at least a quarter century they don't have enough experience to answer the kinds of questions I ask.

This is not meant to exclude people of any gender orientation, skin color, spiritual expression, or other affiliation, but rather it's intended to help you focus on who you think you can help the most at the start. I don't dislike teenagers; they just are not that interested in the kinds of services I offer. In reality, they don't have enough life experience to know how to answer questions like "who are you and what does it all mean?" Someday those questions will be important to them and I will be glad to have that conversation when the time comes.

Your people may include small businesses, government organizations, non-profits, or individuals. Who do you think would benefit from your services?

How would you describe them? What are their habits, frames of reference, or interests? Why would they be attracted to your services?

You Are Unique, But How?

Consultants, trainers, facilitators, and coaches are a dime a dozen in today's marketplace. The average person does not really know how to tell the difference between all the life coaches, leadership consultants, or strategic planners. It's your job to help people see what is different or unique about you.

If you can frame your Superpowers and benefits in a way that others can understand, you are well on your way to demonstrating what is special about you or what distinguishes you from all the other people offering similar services.

The number of consultants in my professional network who say they focus on leadership is astonishing. When I tell people that I wrote a book about leadership, they ask if I have read any number of other books on leadership. To the casual observer, I am just one of thousands of other leadership experts and my book is one of millions on leadership. But my approach to leadership is not the same because my talents and qualifications are unique, as are each consultant and book on leadership.

When speaking to a potential client, it's my job to make the distinctions. In order to help a potential client to decide if I am the best fit for their needs, I need to know who else is playing in the leadership sandbox. They may have started by searching for a leadership consultant, but in the end, they are not hiring services, they are hiring a specific leadership consultant. When you understand how you are distinct from all the other people in your service category, you can guide people to your doorstep.

I make it a point to get to know other consultants in my area. When I meet a new person in the marketplace, I ask them out for lunch. And when a new person contacts me to network, I always accept their invitation. It serves me to know who they are, what their background is, and what they are offering.

Firstly, I may want to refer business to them. I can't satisfy everyone's needs and knowing who else is out there makes me a good resource. The people whom I refer to other consultants never forget that I helped them find a better fit.

Secondly, I want to know who may be competing for the same contract. I ask potential clients if they are shopping around and who else they are talking to. Then I let them know how my approach is different, that my pricing structure is unique, or I reference something unique about my background. When it comes to using the MBTI, for example, I am one of the few people in my area who has written books on Personality Type, and not only attend, but regularly speak at international Type conferences. I am considered a thought leader among my peers, and this helps me stand out when compared to other people using the MBTI.

When I can speak honestly and openly about my competition, potential clients make better informed decisions. Sometimes they choose me, sometimes they don't. I am ok either way because I am committed to them finding the best match for their needs and there may be another time when I may be the better fit.

When looking at possible competitors, start by researching who is in your local market. Unless you already have a large on-line presence, you will likely begin by offering services in your geographic region. At least conduct a cursory Google search to learn who else offers the kinds of services you plan to provide.

Who are some of the consultants in your local area? Do you know them already? What is distinct about what you are offering?

Envisioning The Future

What Compels You Forward?

Having a compelling vision for the future is important because it will help pull you through the daily challenges of being a Solopreneur. It can be lonely and overwhelming in the beginning. There are so many decisions about the logistics and systems you need to get started that it's easy to get lost in the details and lose your focus on what's most important. On any given day, you may become mired in the details of learning a new technology or be overwhelmed when deciding which on-line calendar system to use. If you have a vision for where you are headed, all you need to do is stop and look up. Your vision is always beckoning you forward.

Having a vision for yourself and your company pulls you out of the bog when you get stuck and helps calm you down when your are dissipating into oblivion.

If the word "vision" does not resonate with you, consider your indicators for success. We all have landmarks or mile-markers rolling around in our heads and hearts that let us know when we are on the road to success. What are some of your ideas about what success looks like, feels like, tastes like?

Some of mine included being invited to speak at conferences about my areas of expertise, publishing a book, and hiring a bookkeeper and office assistant so I could be freed from some of the more odious administrative details of running my business. All those things have since happened, and more.

In the middle of it all, I rarely felt like I knew what I was doing. I was often running scared and often got sidetracked every day. I met some goals sooner than others and most looked different than I had anticipated, but I have set and passed many mile-markers in these past decades.

I knew, for example, that I wanted to write and publish a book. I figured there was at least one book inside of me, but at first I did not have a clear focus. When I got clear about my vision, the ideas started flowing.

After coaching people on developing and changing careers, finding their best fit in terms of employment, and helping people launch businesses, it became clear to me that many people were suffering in unsatisfying careers because they didn't understand themselves and seemed unable to effectively obtain jobs that truly suited them.

At the time, I was using some off-the-shelf materials with my career and employment clients and was unsatisfied with them. They were too detailed in areas that didn't matter and not "big-picture" enough where it did matter. I started by adapting some of the materials, and by the third revision of those original materials I had completely transformed the exercises and information into my own.

While I was already working in the field, it was the insight about the source of suffering that helped me connect to my vision. It became clear that I wanted to help end the concept of unemployment and underemployment.

It is my belief that if people actually understood themselves, they would be motivated to leave unsatisfactory jobs and find their best-fitting careers or businesses. Writing a book to help people achieve this while also including tools to help them get suitable jobs was a clear expression of this vision.

My vision was for a future where everyone would be able to fully express their Superpowers while making a living and creating a better world for all.

An important aspect of why people don't understand themselves, by the way, led to my second book. Since I used Personality Type with all my clients, I started noticing some patterns in how different Types recounted their accomplishments. The ones whose Personality Type fit the dominant cultural norms saw themselves as leaders while those whose Types were the most misunderstood by the dominant culture never did.

A large part of what I do is help people tell their stories more clearly, but if they can't see themselves as the leaders that they are, they probably won't apply for higher level positions, advocate for raises for themselves, or be selected to lead teams and projects. Since we have a fairly narrow ideal of what leadership looks and sounds like, the majority of people are passed over when these opportunities arise. I wanted to help people tell their stories more effectively and educate the world about how different styles of leadership can be equally effective.

Again, I was using off-the-shelf materials for Personality Type training and coaching, and I kept having to amend them. At first, I just made some drawings and sketches to demonstrate how different Personality Types lead, then I created a one-page handout, and soon it grew to a few pages. Before I knew it, I had enrolled in a master's program so I would have some structure to do the research. In 2014, I published the first edition of *Leadership Styles*; in 2017, the second; and in 2023, the third.

In the midst of all that writing, I was still running my business, taking care of the daily operations, and having a life. About half-way through my master's program, I nearly divorced my husband. I took a year's break from my studies to mend my marriage. You see, life kept trying to derail me, but my vision for a world where people are able to fully express their Superpowers helped me put one foot in front of the other on the days when little else seemed to make sense.

These days, my indicators, aka goals, include writing books and developing courses that help people discover their Superpowers. They also include more personal lifestyle goals. I have a lovely home and gardens, my husband and I produce 60-70% of our own food, and I have a few grandchildren. I want to maintain my health and well-being so that I can enjoy this life. My indicators also include having a schedule that supports my lifestyle while still generating an income. I am still compelled to create a future where everyone would be able to fully express their Superpowers while making a living and creating a better world for all, I've simply shifted how I am expressing my Superpowers.

You might be thinking that my vision sounds unattainable, and you would be correct if you were thinking on a human scale. It could potentially take many lifetimes to create a future where everyone would be able to fully express their Superpowers while making a living and creating a better world for all. Each time I see the light switch on in a client's eyes or support a team in functioning at a higher level or coach a company owner in building an effective leadership team because they are all tapping into their Superpowers, I'm a little closer. In the process, I know I have inspired others to help create a future where everyone will be able to fully express their Superpowers while making a living and creating a better world for all.

What is your compelling vision? Five years from now, what do you hope to have accomplished, produced, or achieved in your business and personal life?

Serving Your Needs

What Kind Of Rewards Will Make It All Worthwhile?

Ultimately, your business must serve your needs first and foremost. If you are not being rewarded beyond an income, being in business is probably not worth all the effort. Yes, effort. Being in business has many wonderful rewards, but to get them you will have to tap into undeveloped skills, stretch outside your preferences, and overcome yourself daily.

The magic is in creating a business that delivers the rewards that matter while accessing your Superpowers more than half of the time. If you can limit all that tapping, stretching, and overcoming to about 30% of your efforts, you will have the energy for everything there is to do.

As I have said before, I was initially motivated to be an entrepreneur because I didn't want to work for other people. The truth is, I was a terrible employee. In fact, I was fired three times in two years! After my first two attempts in business, Sew Fine and Read Communications, I questioned my ability to be a successful entrepreneur and hid out in some safe jobs. I worked as an office manager, sold advertising for a newspaper, cleaned houses, waitressed, and did a lot of administrative jobs through a temporary employment agency. I was capable of doing all of them and even enjoyed aspects of them. When the temporary agency said they would not place me with another company because I made too many personal calls during work, I hit a low.

I could have gone down many rabbit holes with that kind of track record, but when I was honest with myself about what had happened, I knew I had gotten myself fired because I was too chicken to quit. I was terribly unhappy but didn't have the courage to do anything about it. When I decided to get serious about being in business for myself, I saw it as an opportunity to create a life worth living.

No longer would I be hired or fired at some manager's whim based on another person's idea of how I was supposed to spend my days. I did not want to have to be at the same place at the same time every day and I didn't want to work for people I didn't trust or like.

I wanted to set my own hours, do work that was meaningful to me, and, if I was going to work so dang hard, I wanted to build something that belonged to me. Yes, I was motivated to make money, but I knew there had to be something more I could do than just earn an income.

When I connected with my core motivations (aka my "why"), I started creating the life I wanted and discovered the business model that fit into my life. I wanted a flexible start time, to work with clients and co-workers who I liked and respected, to be able to create, write, and to speak my mind. And if I were going to do any administrative tasks, they would support the functions of my own office.

> *In short, I wanted to own the results of my intellectual, emotional, and physical hard work.*

What kind of a life do you want? Reviewing your motivations may help stimulate some ideas. What changes to your schedule, where you work, or how you work are you seeking? What kind of people do you want to be around? What will you fill your days with that will make it worth taking the risks of being in business for yourself?

A year or two or three from now, how will you know if the effort you have put toward building your business was worth it?

Making a Living

How Much Do You Need to Generate?

Reality check – you have bills and you need to be able to pay yourself! Supporting all the other rewards, making a living from your efforts is essential. If this is the place where you stare into the headlights like a deer, take a moment and just breathe. We are looking at round numbers here. No need to develop a detailed outline of your pricing with weekly sales goals.

Your business may be a source of supplemental income or be your sole income. This may be a side gig for you or a part-time endeavor. All of that is fine but getting an idea of how much income you want to generate will be important later in the process when we look at what you may need to charge for your services.

If you are leaving a full-time job, start with replacing your current income. Or look at your living expenses and create a round number that will allow you to pay your bills. If this is a part-time or side gig, you may have modest expectations. No matter what field you are planning to play on, start putting some numbers on the page.

When I started my business, I was only 26 and had never made much money. I wanted to generate enough income so I could quit my part-time job. It was a low bar, but it gave me something to work toward. Later, the numbers got bigger, but I already knew I could generate sales. When I decided I wanted to generate more, I looked at the services I was offering and made some changes. But I am getting ahead of myself.

If money and budgets make your skin crawl, take a couple of deep breaths, and set this aside for now. You can circle back when you have more information.

If you are comfortable with the numbers, then have at it. No need to get too specific right now. We are still talking round figures.

What kind of income do you need to generate in the beginning to make your Solopreneur enterprise worth your while? How much money would you like to be making in three to five years?

Filling In The Gaps

What Skills And Talents Are Missing?

When you launch your business, you may feel like you are wearing a hundred different hats. That's because you are. But if you step back for a moment, you can toss those hats into three basic rings: Marketing, Operations, and Finance. For example, setting up your technology is part of Operations, figuring out your services and setting prices is Marketing, and setting up your business bank account is part of Finance. Most entrepreneurs are naturally talented in one of these arenas, skilled in another, and sort of a dullard in the third.

Marketing made sense to me in a way that is hard to explain. All the tasks related to developing my services, getting the word out, and enrolling people to engage with me were as easy and natural as drinking water. Operations is a pretty strong skill because I like to be organized and that energy naturally lends itself to setting up office systems. I am not always great, by the way, at maintaining them and often reinvent something because I forgot the system, I created the first time. But remember, this is in the skill area for me. Finance has always been my Bozo area. I understand it and am capable of entering transactions, making deposits, and paying bills, but these are pretty low-level tasks and I resist doing those.

When I became a partner in the small consulting firm where I was subcontracting as a resume writer, my business partner trained me in his basic system and informed me that if I was going to be a part of the business, I had to know how to manage the finances. He knew that this was a weak area for me, but he wasn't about to let me be oblivious.

Over the years, I have developed a lot of skills in all three areas. Some I knew about from the start and many I never knew I would need.

On a side note, when I learned about my Personality Type, it helped me understand more about my Superpowers and Bozopowers.

If you reviewed your list of skills, talents, and qualifications, into which category would the majority of them fall? Are you stronger in Marketing, Operations, or Finance? Which do you think would be beneficial to strengthen?

By the way, you do not need to be masterful at a skill to claim it. There are plenty of tasks I bumble through every day, but I can do them. I am not asking you to rank or evaluate your skills, just to say if you have them or not.

If you are curious about the correlation between your Personality Type and your Superpowers and Bozopowers, take a look at the Appendix for more on Entrepreneur Styles.

Why I Thanked the Man Who Fired Me

It was a low moment in my professional life the day I was fired from a temporary position and then was told by the temporary agency that they would not place me again.

I mean . . . I did make some personal calls, even after my supervisor told me that he could hear me talking to my friend. He was, after all, in the cubicle right behind me. But it wasn't like I didn't do the job for which I was hired. I had worked through the exceedingly long list of calls, updated more files than they imagined possible in the short time I was there, and kept track of my results because it gave me something else to think about besides making calls all day. You try calling hundreds of mechanics and owners of small planes to collect information about the last time they had one of three procedures completed on their engines and tell me you would not have wanted to do almost anything to relieve the boredom!

He called me into the conference room before lunch to tell me that his manager was pressuring him to fire me because I was still making personal calls. I asked for one more chance and went to lunch committed to turning over a new leaf. By the time I returned, he made it clear that I needed to leave immediately.

"No worries," I told myself. "The temporary agency will have a new assignment for me by Monday." No need to tell my boyfriend, with whom I had just moved in three months prior. He would never have to know.

But on Monday, "No, I'm sorry," the woman from the temp agency politely but firmly stated, "We can't place you again."

Apparently, there had been other complaints about my personal call habit.

I was in full-on panic. How was I going to explain getting fired from a *temporary agency*? The only thing to do was get a job before the end of the day.

"That's right," I told myself, "I will get a new job so I will have good news to share tonight."

I managed to convince the tired restaurant manager at a local run-down family diner-type place to not only interview me but hire me on the spot. But the only position he had open was the hostess position that would require me to work the lunch and dinner shift with an inconvenient 3-hour break in the day. I had worked as a waitress and had a low opinion of the hostess position, but I grabbed at that offer like it was gold bullion.

About six months later, my former supervisor from my last temporary worker job walked in. Although this restaurant was only about 5 minutes from his office, he had never ventured in before.

"What is he doing here now?" my mind screeched. Shame overtook my good judgment and I ducked for cover.

After being fired from temporary work, I felt like I had sunk to a new low as a hostess at Lums. There was no way I could show my face in that dining room. Remember, I was the hostess and was supposed to greet people, but I managed to hide in the back for the excruciating 45 minutes he occupied a table.

"Well, that was clever of you," I muttered, feeling proud of dodging that bullet.

When he walked in two weeks later, I knew I could not hide again. It was time for me to confront this demon (not him, my own shame) and vanquish it. We are not given challenges we are not capable of handling, so I knew I had to at least say hello.

"Hi, remember me?" I said as cheerfully as possible.

"Ah . . . yeah," he said cautiously. "How are you?"

"I'm great, actually," I assured him. "You probably don't know this, but after I left your office, the agency refused to place me again."

"Oh, sorry about that," he said nervously.

"No, it's ok. I wanted to thank you for firing me that day. I wasn't happy and needed someone to kick me in the ass so I would make some changes. I had to take a hard look at my life and make some better choices. In addition to working here part-time, I have started two businesses and am happier than I ever was doing temporary work. So, I wanted to thank you for firing me. It was the best thing that happened to me this year."

I never saw him again.

You see, even though I got that hostess job on that fateful day, I knew it was a temporary reprieve. This was a huge wake up call. I hated doing administrative work. I wasn't doing any freelance or creative writing in my off time, and ultimately, I had to confront the fact that I was hiding out. After securing a regular, although paltry, paycheck as a hostess, I started talking to people who knew me. I asked them what they thought I could do; what talents they saw in me that I could put to good use. I felt like I had potential to do almost anything but needed perspective.

I worked at Lums for exactly one year and when I left, I walked into a full partnership in the consulting company I eventually came to own 100%. In and around my weird hostess hours, I made appointments with clients to help them with resumes, cover letters, and their job search. I built a respectable little intrapreneurial enterprise within that firm and proved to myself and everyone else that I was good at something that I liked to do – helping people. When one of the business partners left the firm about 10 months in, the last standing partner offered me 50% ownership of the firm. Within weeks, one of the largest outplacement contracts we had ever won started, and I never looked back.

I am grateful to this day that I got fired from that awful temporary job all those years ago.

Back to the Future

What Is Success?

You already have been thinking about your compelling future and what difference you want to make with clients, now it's time to envision what success looks like for you. Envisioning your future success is about seeing, feeling, hearing, even tasting your own success as a business owner. It's time to get specific.

I remember wanting to wear beautiful clothing, being able to afford nice vacations, being on stage and addressing large crowds, owning a home where I could have a garden and a greenhouse. I wanted to be close to nature and the grocery store. I saw myself walking through my garden every day, writing, teaching, and speaking publicly. I could hear the applause, smell the soil, and feel the fine fabrics against my skin.

I am happy to report that all that and much more is true for me today.

Along the way, I tapped into many undeveloped skills, stretched well outside my preferences, and overcame myself in more ways than I could have imagined. Envisioning my success, having a compelling vision, and being clear about the difference I wanted to make motivated me to overcome all those demons.

Pause for a moment, close your eyes, and imagine yourself five years from now. What do you see, hear, feel, smell? Who is around you? What does your office look like? What kind of home are you inhabiting? You may want to draw a picture, brainstorm some ideas, or make a list of whatever comes to mind. No matter the method, get specific. If you have not gotten clear about the rewards or the difference you want to make or your compelling vision, you can still answer these questions. Allow yourself to imagine in full color.

Now consider the obstacles and barriers that may arise. What are they?

Envisioning your future success is an important aspect of manifesting the life you are seeking by starting your own business. I know you want more than to make enough money to cover your bills. If that is all you wanted, you would get a job, not start a business.

Bringing It All Together

What Are You Offering And Who Is Buying?

We have covered a lot of territory and you probably have a lot of ideas swarming around in your head. I know you don't have answers to all the questions I posed. I also know you know more than you think you do.

It's time to start integrating your ideas and bringing them into form.

Without looking back at any notes, open a fresh page and allow yourself to free write. What kinds of services are you thinking of offering? Who do you think would hire you? Why do you think they would hire you?

Trust yourself, even if all you have done is read this section without answering a single question or writing a single word. If you have gotten this far, you have done more than you realize.

So, take a couple of slow breaths in and out. Pause, and take another slow breath in and out. And write. Or brainstorm on a white board. Or talk things out into a recording device. Or maybe you need to act out some of the answers to our questions. Whatever your process, trust what comes.

No need to look back through all your notes. You know this already. Trust yourself. Let it flow!

Next Steps

Are You A Solopreneur?

Now you are getting an idea of the kinds of services you want to offer, the people who may be interested in engaging with you, and what distinguishes you from others. With those three elements, you have the essential building blocks you need to start your business.

You may be thinking that it can't be that easy, but really it is. If you know who your customers are, you just need to figure out where they are getting their information so you can get in front of them – that's called marketing. If you know how your services are distinct from others and why people will buy from you instead of from other consultants, then you have the core of your marketing message, which will lead to your logo, business cards, website – this is marketing and operations. If you know what you are selling and to whom, you can look at pricing and sales projections. This will lead you into operations and finance. They are all interconnected.

Now it's time to reflect and consider if being a consultant, coach, or other kind of professional service provider is for you.

I have asked you to consider what difference you want to make, the rewards you are seeking, to share your compelling vision, and envision your future. Now ask yourself if being a Solopreneur is for you.

If you know the Solopreneur life is for you, but you need to get a few more ducks in a row, then get those ducks in a row and revisit all of this when you can turn your attention toward it again.

If you have discovered that you are not committed to launching now or ever, this is great news too. Considering the invitation and consciously declining is a powerful step. Hopefully, this process has supported you in gaining clarity.

Remember, you don't have to have it all figured out before starting. Most people in consultative services businesses today didn't start by writing a perfect business plan, don't have fully developed brand strategies with detailed marketing plans, don't have all of their finances in perfect order, and don't keep their websites and social marketing perfectly up to date. And yet, they are still in business, still pay their bills, and are often really happy being in business for themselves, serving their clients, and overcoming the various challenges and obstacles that arise every day.

You too can launch, grow, and prosper as a Solopreneur without having it all sorted.

So, are you a Solopreneur?

2
What are you Selling?
& Who is Buying?

Looks like the answer is *yes*! Yes, you are a Solopreneur! Welcome!

In the previous section we touched on many aspects of your concept and you explored your "why" and the rewards you are seeking. The next phase is to more deeply consider the services you want to offer and the people you want to serve.

In a crowded field of consultants and specialty services, your potential clients and customers need your help. They need help in understanding why they need you to solve their issues, challenges, and problems. This means clearly identifying what you are selling, who your ideal customer is, and how you are different from everyone else. People are inundated with messages, promotions, advertisements, and notifications; the clearer you are about what you are selling and who you want to attract, the easier it will be for you to stand out in the crowd.

Defining your services is the first step. Remember, if you provide a service, your clients are not just buying a generic service, they are buying you as the right person to do the job. While price point is a factor, it is not actually the primary factor in why people will hire you.

Identifying the people who are willing to purchase your product or service at the prices you set is the next step. While your services are fabulous and everyone should want to buy them, not everyone is ready or interested - not everyone needs what you are selling. You are providing a solution to a problem and not everyone has that problem. Start with the most obvious population and build your customer base over time.

When I started offering resume and career services, I didn't need everyone to be my client. I just needed people who needed a resume and wanted a change from their current employment circumstances. These clients are known as job seekers.

It's naive to believe your services are the only or best solution to the challenges your clients face. If you have an idea for a business, there are at least 10 other people who have the same basic idea. How you do it (aka services), how much you charge (aka pricing), who you target in your marketing (aka clients), and where you do it (aka location), are what differentiates you from all the others who claim to have the same solutions. To assist your customers in narrowing their decision to hire you, you must also know who the competition is and how you are different or unique.

There were about five other well-known career counselors and several resume services in my local area when I launched. To the casual observer, I did not necessarily stand out. But once a potential client needed my services and researched the options, they soon discovered I had a different pricing structure and a unique approach to career development than my competitors had. In the beginning I took it personally when a prospective client didn't choose to hire me, but over time I learned to appreciate that my approach was not a fit for everyone.

What Are You Selling?

Describing Your Services

When you reflect on why you want to launch or grow your business, you've already touched upon the nugget of your services. Within your motivations, there is likely a solution you want to provide to an on-going issue you have noticed. This is also known as a gap in the marketplace. Your services will be built around filling that gap. I noticed that folks didn't know how to tell their story in a compelling way and were not getting the jobs for which they were qualified. I approached resume development as if I were writing the branding story of the individual rather than a regurgitation of their employment history.

What is the issue, challenge, or pain you want to alleviate?

When I started, people came wanting a resume or help finding a new job. What they got was a new understanding of themselves, their potential, and their marketability. I didn't just write their resumes, I renovated their stories, helped them identify their priorities and step boldly into better jobs that paid them what they are worth. I provided the opportunities for the growth they were seeking.

If you are just starting, look at what your research revealed. Think about what you imagine or what you intend for people who are seeking your service. Start with what you have and pay attention in your first few years to what actually happens. After a year or two, think about the challenges your clients present to you. What are the changes you witnessed as they accessed your services? What happens to their organizations, teams, lives, careers, health, or finances?

If you have been in business for a while, reflect on why people come to you. What are the challenges they want you to help them resolve? What are the changes you witness as they use your services? What happens to their organizations, teams, lives, careers, health, or finances?

As you develop – or continue to develop – the basic description of your services, incorporate some of the language your clients use. Tell your potential clients what they are getting in exchange for their money. Include the tangible and intangible aspects. Services are a set of tangible and intangible attributes that lead to customer satisfaction; they are bundles of satisfactions that ease discomfort, alleviate ailments, solve problems, create connections.

Start describing your services (ex: training, consulting, coaching, counseling). Include the size, quantity, variety, types, and styles (aka features) and what difference you make with clients (aka benefits). Include how clients can access your services (on-line, in-person, individually, in groups).

Features and benefits are both important. Features help clients compare apples to

Features vs Benefits
- You provide executive coaching services; what you are really selling is peace of mind and opportunity for growth.
- You create books, materials, or webinars; what you are selling is knowledge, insight, resources.

apples; benefits help them understand what is unique about your services and connect more deeply with what is unique about your services.

After understating who your customers are, you will have an opportunity to circle back to take a deeper dive into your services and products. Remember this is not a linear process, so if you don't feel like you finished your services description, let it rest for now. Understanding your customers better will help you clarify your services.

Who's Buying?

Describing Your Customers

Knowing who your people are is the key to attracting and keeping your clients. This will also enable you to identify more clearly who you want to attract with your marketing efforts and help streamline your services, resulting in less struggle, better cash flow, and more personal satisfaction with your business.

Remember not everyone is a potential client. Look at the solutions your services provide and consider what kind of people need those kinds of solutions. If that is too broad, think about who doesn't need or want your solutions. Remember, I don't market to teenagers because they are not usually interested in the core issues that my services address.

Before we go any further, take a moment and free write. Who are your people? What is their ideal age range? What are their hobbies or interests? What level of education do they have? Where do they live? Do they have children or not? Partnered or not? What do they read? Where do they find their information?

You may not know the answers to all these questions and some of them aren't even relevant, but if you think of your clients as three-dimensional beings with real lives, it will make it easier to find them and connect with them. You might also call your ideal client an avatar, your core audience, or primary followers on social media. No matter what you call them, consider both their demographics and psychographics.

I primarily serve professional adults with five or more years of work experience, some post-secondary education, who are seeking to improve their current professional expression. Demographically speaking, my

Demographic vs Psychographic

Demographic descriptors are easily defined by looking at the kind of data the US census collects like age, gender, education level, income, zip code, professions, etc. If your customers are individual people or groups of people these categories will be a good start; if your customers are companies or organizations/institutions then translate this kind of data into business context (yrs. in business, # of employees, type of industry, location, etc.).

Psychographic descriptors include the mindset, habits, interests, activities, and general psychology of your clients or what motivates them to buy your product/service. Think about the challenges, issues, problems you are seeking to address. What kinds of questions do potential clients ask when seeking your services? These are clues to help you understand their mindset.

clients are primarily in their late 20s to early 50s, college-educated, live in the northeastern US, and earn $75,000 or more. Psychographically speaking, my clients are primarily in a professional transition and are seeking to understand themselves and their opportunities better. They also tend to be interested in exploring two core questions: "Who am I? and "What does it all mean?"

This does not mean I don't serve people outside of these factors, it just means I don't spend any resources marketing my services to them. I actually have a long-term contract to support a lot of young professionals who have little to no experience. I provide a variety of professional development training, coaching, and consulting to several hundred AmeriCorps members throughout Vermont, every year.

But I did not pursue that population. A professional colleague referred me to the state-wide training coordinator for AmeriCorps members in Vermont because they needed someone to provide a workshop on a topic that my colleague did not provide. That was in the early 2000s and I have been providing a wide variety of workshops, coaching, and consulting services to the members ever since.

Although AmeriCorps has been one of my longest standing clients, I still don't consider the members to be primary clients. Firstly, it is the state-wide organization that actually hires me; the members are end users. Secondly, I mostly provide what I call technical assistance to the members, like how to write a resume and look for a first job. While I provide this technical assistance to all my clients, it is a small part of what I provide for older professionals; it is not the actual core of my services.

AmeriCorps members are what I define as secondary clients. They are a lot like my primary clients (college educated, live in the Northeast) but are missing some key elements (age and experience). When a member seeks me out years after their service has ended, they become a primary customer: by then they are in their late 20s, have about five years of experience, and are interested in discovering who they are and what it all means.

If you have been in business for a few years or more, use your historical data to describe your clients. If you are just starting, use your educated guestimate of who your clients are.

Who are your people?

Expanding Menu of Services Based on the Same Core Benefit

Quite by accident, I built a business that includes a variety of services that allows me to prosper through the boom-and-bust cycles in the economy. When unemployment is low, more private individuals come knocking because they feel confident about finding another suitable position or they want to start a business. When unemployment is high, outplacement services are suddenly in demand because companies release their once precious employees back into the wild. Through it all, I have a consistent level of corporate training and consulting that keeps my calendar as full as I want it to be.

All of my services start from the same core benefit: helping people create the lives they really want to be living. No matter if I am coaching a woman returning to the workforce after being home with young children, facilitating a senior leadership team in a strategic planning session, or leading a job search and interviewing workshop for a group of people who have been laid off, I am always providing coaching, tools, and exercises that assist people in figuring out what they really want, guiding them in articulating it in such a way that others can understand it, and taking the initial steps toward manifesting that vision.

I started by providing career counseling and job search coaching because that was the most natural place for me. I was already interested, had some natural talent, and was motivated to learn more. Outplacement services are a natural extension. When an employer lays off one or hundreds of people, they have an option to provide those people with career and job search coaching, aka outplacement. Private career services and outplacement services are essentially the same service with the same end user. The customer, as in who is paying the bill, is the only difference. The employer pays for the outplacement services.

I use different wording and present my services in a slightly different light for each of these customers because they have different needs, but I use the same exact materials for a private pay client as I do for an outplacement client.

Entrepreneurial coaching was also a natural outgrowth of the career services. I occasionally had clients who decided that what they really wanted was to start a business. I began by speaking from my experience and that seemed to help. I discovered that I really liked helping people start businesses, especially professional consulting services. My instincts were good, but I needed more technical resources.

In the mid-1990s, I was recruited to teach the Personal and Professional Development (PPD) section of a team-taught course designed to assist women in developing and launching entrepreneurial endeavors. Although my primary subject was the PPD curriculum, I had several years of experience in owning and growing my own business and often shared my personal insights, marketing tips, and observations with the class. When the Marketing instructor was transitioning off the team, I made a pitch to teach that section and stepped into a new role.

After teaching for the Women's Small Business Program(WSBP) for five years, I was serendipitously recruited to teach a marketing course at the New England Culinary Institute (NECI). I was an adjunct instructor at NECI for five years in their Bachelor of Arts program for Food and Beverage Management and taught a variety of courses including business concept development, marketing research, and leadership/management courses. I also co-taught the capstone project course, in which students had to come together as a functioning team and work collaboratively on a "real-time" project for a local company or organization related to the food and beverage industry.

This last course was the hardest to teach and my favorite. Since the students in the BA program were a small cohort and I taught a variety of other courses throughout their program, I knew them well and we had formed mutual trust. My co-teacher, who happened to be the Assistant Dean, was also an excellent facilitator and our styles were highly complementary. After teaching that course five times together, we had developed great materials and tangible results. Later, I was able to translate all of what I learned into corporate contracts.

After teaching at WSBP and NECI, I left with a deep understanding of how to create curricula and course materials, a pile of instructional materials and books, and 10 years of experience in teaching entrepreneurism from many different angles to people from a wide variety of backgrounds. As a result, I developed a program for entrepreneurial coaching that continues to evolve today.

The training and consulting with organizations came later, but it was also a natural outgrowth of the individual services and the teaching experience. My primary individual clients are experienced professionals between 35 and 60 years old. Many of these folks were in leadership roles and respected my approach to professional development and the insights I provided. When these same people were re-employed, they brought me inside to help improve their teams, create professional development programs, and to coach individual employees.

Throughout all this time, I also became certified in various tools like the Myers-Briggs Type Indicator (MBTI) and Emotional Intelligence (EQ), completed a Master's program in Leadership and Group Dynamics, and took various workshops in facilitation, mediation, and coaching. Simultaneously, my partner was transitioning into more corporate training and often brought me in to lead the MBTI sessions. I liked the variety of interaction that the groups brought, and it turns out I was pretty good at leading these sessions.

I made my first big break into training when I was referred to a local business that was experiencing growing pains and I convinced the owner that I could help him sort out the difficult dynamics so that he could grow his business while creating a strong corporate culture of team and collaboration. I had been inside of a lot of companies to present several workshops by this time, but this was my first real contract to facilitate the team development over a three-year period.

So, you see, I am still providing the same benefit to my clients, but now I have more ways to ease their pain. I have had to learn how to pitch this benefit in many different forms, based on my audience, but I know that what I do every day is help people create the lives they really want to be living and get on with living them.

Who is Your Competition?

Defining How You Are Distinct

When you know who your competition is you can more effectively market your services to your primary clients. Remember every consulting, coaching, and professional services business sounds like every other consulting business to the casual listener. In order to capture and keep the attention of potential clients, you need to be able to make distinctions between you and all the other people offering similar sounding services. Additionally, knowing your competitors enables you to collaborate and refer business to each other when opportunities arise.

Competition comes in many forms; some are obvious, and some are not. For example, I offer live workshops using the Myers Briggs Type Indicator. If I am looking for my obvious competitors, I might search for other consultants offering Myers Briggs related training and consulting. But if I am thinking broadly, I need to include consultants who offer any kind of personality style training. This can include consultants who use the DiSC system, Emotional Intelligence, Strengths Finder, and the Predictive Index. But I also need to include pre-recorded training, books, and any website offering this kind of information, in addition to all the other lesser-known tools available that help people learn about how groups of people interact and that can improve their performance.

My direct competition can be defined as narrowly as other MBTI practitioners or as widely as all consultants who use any kind of framework for understanding people. My indirect competition includes all the resources available online, books, and even internal employees who seem to be able to understand people.

If you are serving individuals consider as resources other coaches and consultants in your area and online, but also include other available sources that claim to offer similar results.

A long-standing indirect competitor to my career services is the book *What Color is Your Parachute* by Richard Bolles and Katherine Brooks (Ten Speed Publishing). It has been in publication since before I was in business and is regularly updated. The book promises to guide individuals through a comprehensive career exploration process and help them build a better career.

> ### Direct vs Indirect Competitors
>
> **Direct Competitors:** services and business that offer what you offer. At first glance you may assume you have little to no competition but remember that most of your potential customers do not know you yet and what you offer may sound a lot like what other consultants or service providers offer.
>
> **Indirect Competitors:** services and businesses that vie for the same funds or resources that your customers spend on your products/services. (Ex: "free webinars," out of town consultants, books, in-house employees with some similar skills or certifications) This category of competition can be more challenging to identify, but try searching for some key terms on the internet to get some ideas.

Several years into being in business, I noticed that several potential clients mentioned buying the book, getting through the first few chapters, and becoming overwhelmed. The self-directed nature of the book only took them part of the way before they needed a live person to help them with the rest of the process. Years later, I discovered a state-by-state directory of career counselors in the back of that book. There were no career counselors listed for Vermont and it was free to be listed. Every couple of years I receive a verification from Ten Speed Press, the publisher, asking me to update my contact information.

You can use any number of factors to compare your business to another. Some common items include type and variety of services and products, price point, level of expertise, image, reputation, quality, customer service, reliability, location, sales approach, and availability.

When starting this inquiry, it's best to focus on direct competitors in your general geographical region. If you discover a new potential competitor, add them to your research. You can fall down a lot of rabbit holes researching your direct and indirect competition. There is no need to complete a comprehensive comparison. Just get enough useful information to help you make informed decisions. There are better activities on which to spend your time.

Who are your competitors? Take a moment now to consider what kinds of services may be competing for the same client base, may offer similar results, or provide "free" advice in your field.

Which elements of your services are unique or distinct from your direct competitors? How might you frame those differences when speaking to a potential client?

Good Competitive Practices

Get to know your direct and indirect competitors: Join relevant professional associations. This will help you more clearly identify how to distinguish your business and services when talking to potential customers.
- Meet with professionals who you know 1 to 1 and pick their brains.
- Attend their public workshops or conference presentations to see them in action.
- Ask people who have used their services about their experience.
- Always accept invitations from other consultants (new or established) to network - you never know where these conversations will lead.

Develop collegial, collaborative relationships with competitors: This positions you well to grow your business through your strengths

Partner with competitors on larger contracts.
- Refer business to people who more clearly meet a potential customer's needs.
- Receive referrals from people who see that you clearly meet a potential customer's needs.

Conduct regular competitive research: This helps you to keep it real and continually challenge yourself.
- This helps you keep it real and continually challenge yourself.
- Revisit your competitive analysis chart every few years to monitor how you are growing and how your competition may have changed.
- Pay attention to who is doing business with whom.
- Listen carefully to feedback from satisfied and dissatisfied customers.

Engender a spirit of generosity: This will always serve you and help you be experienced by clients as a true professional among professionals.
- This will always serve you and help you be experienced by clients as a true professional among professionals.
- Speak well of competitors and make clear distinctions between what they offer and what you offer.
- Be a resource to fellow members and associates of professional organizations. Everyone benefits when consultants raise the professionalism bar.

Friendly Competition

When I was a newcomer in my local market, I sought out the people who were already established consultants and coaches. I wanted to connect, learn about their background, and look for ways we could collaborate. Most were kind enough to meet with me and when we saw each other in professional and social circles, we chatted, but not much more.

There were two women, however, who did more. Both had been in business for about 10 years. They happened to share an office space where they had developed a symbiotic relationship that allowed for collaboration when needed and independence when desired. I was not the first newcomer to come knocking.

Throughout the years, the three of us occasionally included each other on large outplacement proposals or RFP responses to the State. While only a few of those proposals were ever accepted, the process opened new channels for connection. Yes, we were still technically competitors, but we understood we didn't have to be competitive with each other. We knew there was plenty of work for all of us.

Most of my local market competitors who dominated the market when I started, have long since retired or moved on to other pursuits. I have become one of the "old timers" and now new people seek me out.

I have always made time to meet with people who are interested in offering career and employment services because I know something good will come from it. Some of those newcomers have joined my business as contract consultants or collaborated on a project with me, some joined other consultant groups, and many have launched their own practices. In the end, we all benefited from our connection.

Beyond any possible collaboration, however, there are some very practical reasons for me to make the time to have lunch or coffee with these folks. I need to know who my competition is now and in the future. I need to understand what their strengths are and how to differentiate myself from them in the marketplace.

My best competitive edge is knowing my strengths and their strengths. When meeting with a potential client, I always ask if they are shopping around. If they are shopping, I suggest some questions to ask and explain how my services and style are unique in the marketplace. I educate potential clients on becoming savvy consumers and occasionally even refer them to another consultant. Sometimes they choose me and sometimes they select a different provider to meet their needs.

This may seem counter-productive, but it's not. I want potential clients to come to me first, knowing I will honestly represent my services. I have built my reputation as a consultant on being a trusted advisor and it's vital that I maintain my integrity.

People who offer the same or similar services are not your enemies. They are part of a network or field of energy that you can tap into when needed. Establishing and maintaining a dynamic field of professional colleagues will bring you many more returns than diminishing your competitors ever will.

Finding What's Special

Defining Your Unique Selling Proposition

Discovering that you're offering something unique is the first step; now it's time to translate what's special into language that will make a difference to a potential client, aka your Unique Selling Proposition (USP). You need three ingredients to create an effective USP: a clear description of your services, an understanding of who your audience is, and the distinction of yourself from the competition. If you have at least attempted to answer all the questions presented so far, you have the raw materials to your USP.

Review your notes and pull out the core needs your services are intended to meet. List a few ways that you meet that core needs. Next list a couple of your primary competitors and how you distinguish yourself from them. What are some reasons that your company will be successful?

Developing Your Elevator Pitch

Now comes the translation. Converting what makes your services unique into a marketing message is known as *writing your elevator pitch*. An elevator pitch is what you say in response to the question: "What do you do?" when promoting your professional services at a networking event, when someone contacts you, or when you need to explain your business to your relatives. It's basically several sentences that help another person understand who you are, what you do, what you are interested in doing and how you can be a resource to your audience within the time it takes to ride in an elevator from the first to fifth floors.

Having a clear elevator pitch enables people to understand when and how to hire your services, to whom you can be referred, and how to represent you to others.

Lacking a good Elevator Pitch often results in ineffective referrals and the attraction of undesirable clients that take up your precious time and energy.

Features help clients compare apples to apples. My own elevator pitch might be, "Hi, I am Markey Read with MRG, Inc and I offer a variety of business consulting services, including leadership and team development."

> *Benefits help others understand what is unique about your services and connect more deeply with what is unique about them: "Hi I am Markey Read with MRG, Inc and I help small companies move through the stages of growth with grace and humor. I do this by collaborating with owners to develop their leadership team and access the Superpowers of their people."*
>
> *What I say to my family: "I help people get along better and be more productive."*

Features Tell, Benefits Sell

KNOW YOUR AUDIENCE- Before writing any part of your introduction, consider your audience. You will be much more likely to succeed if your elevator pitch is clearly targeted at the individuals to whom you are speaking. Having a "one-size-fits-all" elevator pitch is almost certain to fail.

You may need one version for general inquiries, another for your referral group, and another for your relatives and friends.

KNOW YOURSELF - Before you can convince anyone of your proposition you need to know exactly what it is. You need to define precisely what you are offering, what problems you can solve and what benefits you bring to a prospective contact or client.

If you haven't looked at your competition, take some time to do that now.

PROMOTE BENEFITS NOT FEATURES – Benefits Sell, Features Tell. Remember: your services alleviate a pain point.

Time to Create Your Business Roadmap

It may seem like you are answering the same questions over and over again . . . and you are, sort of. But this is an important part of the process.

If you simply copy and paste the same text over and over again, you are missing the point. The more you question your assumptions, reconsider your initial ideas, and allow your mind to percolate on these main components of your business, the more likely you are to discover what you are really selling, who is really buying, and how you are truly distinct from all the other people who offer something similar to the same population. Remember, the general population really does not understand how consultants can make a difference and therefore may assume that one consultant is as good as another.

So, prepare your favorite hot beverage and without referring to anything you previously wrote, use the one-page business plan on the following page. Fill in as many areas as you can. When you are done, compare this to your answers to the same questions in the last chapter.

What parts of your concept areas are clearer?

What parts are less clear?

What areas do you still need to develop?

What questions do you have now?

Business Roadmap

Service/Product Mix
(what are you selling?)

Customer/Client
(who is your target audience?)

Market Size
(how many potential clients exist in your desired location?)

What is the primary problem, challenge, issue that you want to help people or organizations with?

Marketing & Promotion
(how will you communicate with your target audience?)

Competition
(who else provides this service? list 3-5)

Competitive Advantage
(how are your services different?)

Gross Sales
(annual sales target)

Personal Fit
(how will you know if Solopreneurship is for you?)

Hourly Rate
(gross sales/1000 hrs.)

Current Obstacles
(what don't you know or have available to start?)

Daily Rate
(gross sales/100 days)

3
How Do I Make a Living?

Pricing is one of the trickiest parts of launching and growing a business. There are so many factors such as what you need to charge to make a living, what you think your clients are willing to pay, and what your competitors are charging. The hardest factor to resolve, however, is what you think your services are worth.

Remember price is not the primary factor in why people will hire you. Yes, you will encounter people who say they can't afford your services, but those folks may not be your primary clients. This is why understanding who your clients are is key to establishing your pricing levels.

Simply put, you can charge whatever people are willing to pay for your products and services. The better you understand your customer base, have described your services, and can distinguish yourself from the competition, the more likely you will find the sweet spot in pricing that allows you to make a comfortable living while connecting to your clients in a meaningful way by providing solutions to the challenges they face. A solid pricing strategy reflects the company image, exists in the context of the marketplace, and meets the needs of customers by providing quality services and a rate your customers agree is good value.

Pricing Your Services

Determining your pricing strategy is more than covering your costs and paying your bills. Yes, you need to know your costs and cover them, but costs and price are independent. Customer decisions are based on quality, service, price, and your ability to meet their expectations. What you charge indicates the level of service clients can expect; their expectations are reflected in their psychographics and demographics. If you are charging top dollar for your services, for example, you may attract high-end clients, but you must also give high-end service.

Start by learning what your direct competitors charge for the same or comparable services. Assess the perceived value of what you offer compared to what your competitors offer. What are the tangible and intangible differences? What's the image you are portraying?

Start higher than you think is justified and let the marketplace guide you. It's much easier to lower your prices than to raise them. The marketplace will let you know if you are charging too much, but it will never say your prices are too low.

In the beginning, I used several methods to research my competitor's prices. Firstly, I listened carefully to my clients. Some people were refugees from my competitor's services, others were shopping and told me how my prices compared. I occasionally asked my competitors when it seemed appropriate. And when I was expanding my services to include corporate outplacement, I hired a marketing researcher who helped me understand the landscape and set my prices.

So, What Should I Be Charging?

Yes, you can charge whatever people are willing to pay for your products and services. While this is not intended to give you permission to gouge or cheat clients you have complete and utter permission to make a living and make a profit.

Pricing for consultants and other professional service-based businesses is particularly challenging because your rates will likely shock people at first. Their minds quickly run amok calculating 40 hours X 52 weeks X your hourly rate and conclude that you are at least a millionaire and possibly a billionaire. Firstly, consultants rarely bill 40 hours a week, 52 weeks of the year. Secondly, that hourly rate must cover a variety of expenses that are necessary but cannot be billed to a client.

> ### General Principle – Seek the Highest Possible Prices
> There is nothing illegal, unethical, or immoral in seeking the highest price for your services that the market is willing to pay.
> **Pricing your services too low is one of the common reasons for business failure.**

Common False Assumptions in Pricing

Assumption	Why it's counter productive
I can charge less than my competition.	Larger enterprises have more leeway with pricing and can underbid a project because they have more projects or staff or can withstand longer periods of little or no profit than Solopreneurs.
I will set my prices low until I gain experience (especially when the owner is providing the service.)	You run the risk of sending a message of being a bargain or of not being able to provide the same quality. This can trap you into a lower price range than you desire in the long haul.

Bring Your Value to Pricing

In order to shift the focus away from what you are charging, you need to educate your clients. Help them understand what your rates include and build in value wherever you can.

A daily rate of $3,000, for example, may seem high when out of context. For every hour of a workshop I present, however, I log at least four to six before even arriving at a client site. There is the obvious time in planning the session with the client, preparing the materials, creating a slide deck, and traveling to the site. There are many hours that I cannot include on an invoice.

When submitting a proposal for potential corporate consulting and training, I always mention that my daily rate includes all preparations for the training, delivering the training, and any follow up meetings. My "daily rate" is essentially equal to what it costs me in time to show up and be ready to go at a client site.

I also spend money and time participating in professional development workshops and conferences, maintaining certifications, and creating new products. I can't really charge clients for all that, but I can let them know I make that kind of investment to bring high value to their workshop.

Many years ago, I had a client who was unhappy with my pricing after I had completed a series of training sessions and submitted the invoice. Although we had discussed my daily rate and the per person materials fees, he had not taken into consideration the additional costs when he added 15 more people to the workshops. He was surprised by the total. He questioned the price of the materials, saying they were "just copies," and wanted me to adjust the invoice.

I explained that what he called copies were licensed materials that I had permission to reproduce. I further explained that I had paid for that permission, including the initial certification training, and the on-going continuing education to maintain that permission. The materials fee was an intellectual property fee, not a printing fee.

In the end, he paid the invoice and when we did business in the future, he treated me with more respect.

Project, Daily, and Hourly Rates

Even if you don't charge by the hour, I recommend that you establish an hourly rate because it will enable you to calculate your daily and project fees more effectively.

No matter what your pricing strategy, start by setting an annual income goal. Estimate your annual sale goals by totaling your operating expenses, salary, and desired profit. (Remember this is a goal, a target to aim for, to be used as a guide throughout the year. It's based on your best calculations, but it's not written in stone.) Then, break it into quarterly, monthly, weekly, and daily increments to help you monitor your progress.

When I started using this method, I kept my daily, weekly, monthly, and quarterly goals on a 5x8 index card next to my computer. At the end of each month and quarter, I totaled my billable hours and income (cash sales and invoiced sales) and tracked the total against my goals. It helped me get a feel for what kind of pace I needed to maintain to meet my goals.

If you further reduce your goals to an hourly rate, you will be able to price your project and daily rates more accurately. Keep in mind, however, that you cannot bill for 40 hours a week. Full-time consulting usually equates to billing 20 hours a week or 1,000 hours annually, (based on 20 hours/week, for 50 week/year). When you launch, plan on 10-12 hours of actual billed time for more realistic planning. The rest of the time is for marketing, responding to messages, bookkeeping, managing technology, professional development, travel, and all the other tasks and activities that consume your time.

To determine project-based pricing, observe the average number of hours you spend delivering various services or completing types of projects and use the 1,000 hours of billable time to determine how many of those projects you can realistically deliver in a year. Then divide your annual goal by the number of projects and you'll get a fairly good idea of your project-based price.

For daily rates, translate the 1,000 hours into approximately 3 days a week of billable time, or 156 days a year, and divide your annual gross sales goal by 156. A full day is not necessarily eight hours of billable time. If you are delivering a workshop, for example, you may be on site for eight hours, but plan to provide six hours of actual content.

Establishing an hourly rate, by the by, helped me price the programs and show the real value. If an individual client does the math, they will see that the program gives them access to my time at a 15-20% discount from the hourly rate.

Basic Pricing Formula:
Price = Labor + Expenses + Materials + Overhead + Profit

Your Hourly, Daily, and Project Fees Need to Cover:

- Your salary, taxes, and benefits (including vacations, sick days, and saving for retirement).
- Professional development (maintaining certifications, staying current in your field).
- Research and development (developing new products and services),
- Overhead expenses (office equipment and supplies, rent, profit - Yes, it's a good thing to plan for a profit).
- Bad debt (clients who don't pay - it's rare, but unavoidable for most service businesses at some point).
- Time spent on marketing and general administration of the business.
- Plus, the value you bring to your clients!

Two Simple Methods for Determining Your Rates:

Based on Annual Sales Goal ($100,000)

➢ Average Annual Billable time = 1,000 hrs.
➢ Average hourly rate = $100/hr.
➢ Average 10 hours per project = 100 projects/yr.
➢ Project-based fee = $1,000/project
➢ Average number of billable days/wk.
➢   = 3 (165 days/yr.)
➢ Daily Rate = $600/day

Based on Personal Salary Goal ($50,000)

➢ Double $50,000 = $100,000
➢ Divide by 1000 hours = $100/hr.
➢ Average 10 hours per project = 100 projects per year
➢ Project-based fee = $1,000/project
➢ Average number of billable days/wk. = 3 (165 days/yr.)
➢ Daily Rate = $600/day

Super Simple Method for Determining Your Annual Sales Goal:

Estimate your desired salary (aka personal income) and double that number.

Reality Check

These formulas are intended to help you get useful information; they are not intended to be strictly followed. If your goal is to generate $500,000 annually in your first year, your hourly rate would need to be $500. Unless you are extremely well known in your field or live in an alternate universe, it is unlikely that you will fill 10 to 20 hours a week at $500 an hour in your first year.

I encourage you to play with these numbers, get comfortable with the formulas, and use them to understand how to frame your services. Start as high as you want, run the numbers, and do a reality check.

> *I believe your prices should always make you a little nervous in the beginning, but not terrify you.*

Throughout the years I have assessed and raised my prices multiple times. Each time I run the numbers, then let them sit for a couple of weeks, look at them again, and then test them. When I finally broke the $100 per hour level, I remember quoting my new prices to a few prospective clients, who quickly ended the conversation. They said they couldn't afford my services. I let my fears rule the day and retreated to my previous level. Six months later, I reimplemented the new prices and no one seemed to notice.

I learned two important lessons. Firstly, those few prospects who said they couldn't afford my services were not really in my primary client group and I placed more importance on their reactions than was warranted. Secondly, I was a little terrified of those new prices and my mind ran amok. I was so uncomfortable, bordering on terror, that I couldn't "sell" the new prices confidently. I am not sure what changed six months later; I was just finally ready.

These days, when an individual client wants to enroll in a program but flinches at the price, I address it straight on. I ask, "Is this program financially feasible for you?" Then I emphasize that my services are an investment in their future by saying "I will teach you to fish for the rest of your life, instead of giving you a fish every week during the program." If it's a matter of cash flow, I suggest breaking up the total amount into two or three payments. If a client needs smaller increments, I require one-third up front, as a show of commitment. Then we make an agreement for the remainder, as long as the balance is paid by the last appointment.

Notice, I don't ask, "Can you afford it?" or "What do you want to pay?" I help them overcome the obstacle without reducing my prices. It's a win-win.

Please use the formulas. Run your numbers and run some more. Play with this process. When you can fully embody your prices, you will be able to stand confidently in them and people will gladly pay you what you are worth.

Create An Hourly Rate
Even If You Never Charge By The Hour

Hourly rates are useful when someone wants to pick your brain or get your perspective in an area of your expertise. You don't have to charge when people want to "pick your brain," but I promise you that there will be times when you will want to charge.

When I am meeting with a peer, colleague, or friend, and they want to pay me, I usually just ask them to pick up the lunch tab. These conversations deepen my relationships with these folks and widen my potential referral network. It also gives me permission to pick the brains of people I respect.

If someone asks for a lot of my time or has some kind of hidden agenda, however, I can always choose to charge them. This usually discourages the person from abusing my time. If they are willing to pay, then it's at least some consolation for dealing with them.

And there are times when meeting with a client for an hour or two can make all the difference for them and they insist on paying you. Having an hourly rate handy can generate some additional income.

Since the start, I have offered professional development coaching and consulting to individuals at various income levels. For many years, I only offered flat fee programs for job search, career development, and entrepreneurial development. I didn't offer hourly services for the first ten years because I wanted people to enroll in the programs where we could dig deeper and make more progress.

There were always clients who didn't need the full program and would still benefit from a couple of hours to prepare for an interview, discuss a job offer, or address an unfortunate professional situation. Since most of these folks were referred to me, I often felt obliged to help. When the exceptions became the norm, I added hourly services to my menu of options.

Establishing an hourly rate, by the by, also helped me price the flat fee programs more effectively by showing the real value. If a client does the math, they will see that my programs give them access to my time at a 15-20% discount from my normal hourly rate.

After adding an hourly option, I did not market it. At all. Hourly services are an example of a tertiary service. I accept the flow when it arrives, I help people as much as possible, and am grateful for the income. A few of those folks enroll in more comprehensive services, but most do not.

Project Rates

Project or flat fees are useful when you provide a service that is more akin to a product than a service. You may be an expert at developing and implementing digital marketing plans, for example, and you charge a monthly rate to manage the project. You may be an editor and charge a flat rate per page.

Flat rates are based on how long it takes you to accomplish the task and your income goals. If you want to generate $2,000 a week and you expect to bill for 20 hours of your time per week you need to know how many of those projects it takes to fill 20 hours of billable time per week and charge accordingly.

Flat fees are easier to establish and are more common for experienced consultants because the more times you have delivered a particular result the more likely you are to have a sense of how long it takes to deliver. Flat fees, however, are more than the sum of number of hours it takes to deliver; they are also based on the value the service brings to your clients.

To start, figure your pricing based on number of hours. If you don't know how long it takes you to do various frequent tasks, start tracking your time. While this may seem tedious, it will give you valuable information. If you are one of those people who moves several projects forward simultaneously and the idea of tracking your time feels overwhelming, I encourage you to conduct an experiment for a couple or a few months. Pay attention to your level of productivity for a few months and you will get a fairly good idea of how many hours you spend to deliver on a project.

As you gain experience, you also gain speed and increase quality. As you get faster, better, more efficient, charging a flat fee means getting paid for results or value, not the hours logged.

Another approach to project or flat fee pricing is to give clients an estimated range, based on a proposal. The low end would be for the basic level of the proposal, the high end would include all the bells and whistles. The final invoice will likely be somewhere in the middle. This approach helps accommodate project creep.

Many clients prefer flat fees because they can budget for it and there are no unexpected costs.

Daily Rates

Daily rates are in an entirely different realm and are generally used in the context of long-term contracts and projects. You may be hired, for example, to deliver a series of workshops or an established curriculum.

Daily rates are also used by consultants who establish an on-site presence for an agreed upon time period to perform various tasks. They may be launching a team and providing on-site management until the team is fully operating or managing a project involving multiple departments that is eased by your presence.

Be aware that daily rates are highly susceptible to sticker shock. Remember, a daily rate for training needs to cover all the pre and post meetings with the client, your preparation time, travel to and from the site, and all the miscellaneous bits necessary to deliver quality workshops.

For every day of training delivered, plan on spending one to two days preparing. Even if you have presented the materials dozens of times, you will likely update or customize your slides

Beware Project Creep

The risk you take as a consultant is managing your time and staying alert to project creep. If you are not as productive as you planned, you will likely lose money or not meet your income projections. If this is a regular occurrence, take a look at what you are charging to make some adjustments.

Flat fee pricing is highly susceptible to project creep especially when the project is not clearly defined, the client does not really know what they want, or you do not keep your boundaries in place. Clients are usually overly optimistic about how little time or effort will be required to accomplish the desired result and therefore, shop around for a quick fix or place unrealistic expectations on a consultant's ability to motivate their employees to be more wonderful, productive, and communicative than they are at the moment.

Projects can quickly morph mid-stream and you can find yourself logging a lot more hours than expected and making a lot less money than projected. If you use project-based fees, expect, and anticipate project creep. Establish a process for what a carpenter or plumber would call a "change order".

Since your clients rarely call your attention to when a project starts to morph, you can catch it early by monitoring your hours. Take note of the extras and be careful not to give away too much just to "keep the gig." If you talk about the potential for creep in the beginning, it is easier to address it mid-stream.

Beware Project Creep (cont.)

I offer various flat fee entrepreneurial and professional development coaching programs that include 10 appointments and all related materials. Clients can also ask quick questions between sessions. Even though they are paying for 10 appointments and materials, I budget about 13 hours of total time and price the program accordingly. Most people do not exceed the 13 hours and about 25% ask questions via texts and emails between meetings.

When a client starts asking me complex questions that will take me longer than five minutes to answer by email, I suggest that we either set a special appointment to discuss them or include them in our next scheduled time. Additionally, when a client wants to continually edit and change their resume document, I let them know that since they have the master document, they are welcome to continue to make changes because it is a living document and I do not need to see all the changes. I not only remind them that they have ownership of their document, but I also set a healthy boundary for myself.

Another form of project creep rears its ugly head in workshops and group meetings. When leading a training session or facilitating a workshop, I plan the presentation to match the time frame, accounting for enough time to complete and debrief exercises and answer questions throughout. Occasionally, I have a participant who either wants to debate the legitimacy of the basic premises I am using or asks questions that will take me too far off course.

To curtail this tendency, I have a few basic ground rules that I state at the start of any workshop or presentation. First, I say, "You can ask me any question that comes to mind, when it comes to mind". I know that I sometimes dawdle on a slide for longer than necessary and their questions often prompt me to move along. If someone asks a question that relates to a later portion of the material, I respectfully ask them to hold their question until we get to that part.

In every workshop, however, someone wants to ask a related but divergent question. To accomplish this, after letting them know they can ask any question, at any time, I also say, "If your question will take us down a rabbit hole, we can talk at the break". This lets them know that they are free to ask anything and that I am free to either not answer it or that we can discuss it at another time.

For corporate consulting projects, I always include hourly coaching in my proposals. This gives me the flexibility to invoice for meetings that are beyond the basic planning and debriefing related to the project.

I regularly make exceptions and break my own guidelines based on various elements. Since I have established the boundaries at the start, however, it is easier for me to nudge a client toward the guidelines when needed. I am managing the project, not the client.

or materials for each client.

Since people who hire you do not usually conduct training sessions and workshops, they often have no concept of what it means to show up at 8 am ready to start; you can help them appreciate the real value of your time. As part of the proposal and invoicing stages, I list all the items included in the daily rate.

If an organization has budgetary limits for training, look for other ways to be compensated for the preparation. As I've mentioned, I provide a considerable number of professional development workshops for the State of Vermont's AmeriCorps organization, and because it's a federally funded program, there are many strange restrictions on what they can and cannot pay for. Their budgeting system parses out multiple subcategories of allowable expenditures, however, so I have collaborated with the woman who manages the contacts to figure out how to invoice for all of my time. Turns out they have a category for preparation, so I charge "by the hour" for the equivalent of a day for preparation and then charge a daily rate for the workshops. In the end, I do not make my full "daily rate" for training, but I make more money than if hadn't asked for assistance.

If your daily rate is an obstacle, collaborate with your client. If you have established your value and know your pricing is fair, ask if they pay for preparation time separately than delivery time and simply split your daily rate between the two. Ask if they prefer to fold materials fees into the daily rate or have another way of accounting for them.

The larger the organization, the more complex their budgeting process is. Non-profits, municipal, state, and federal government agencies tend to have convoluted levels of tracking expenditures because they are accountable to funders and/or taxpayers. Large corporations with multiple divisions can be equally complex for different reasons. If you don't ask a few simple questions, you could be losing opportunities to get paid for what you are worth.

Retainers & Other Pricing Structures

Retainers, equity, deferred income, and a percentage to sales are other ways you can structure your pricing, but these are less common and introduce a level of complexity that new Solopreneurs should approach with great caution.

Retainers are essentially a weekly or monthly fee that a client pays to have access to you. This may be unlimited or may have some conditions. For example, you may offer up to 10 hours a month and a client can use up to 120 hours in a year. This is a common practice among legal and financial advisors. You could also open the floodgates and say you will make yourself available to a client within a reasonable amount of time. Most clients will not abuse this kind of access; those that do can be migrated out of your client list when you renegotiate contracts.

Being paid in the form of equity means you are receiving some shares of stock or percentage of ownership in a company. This is more common in metropolitan areas awash in high-risk start-ups that are seeking venture capital. These companies are usually planning to grow fast and get bought by a larger company, allowing the owners to cash out. The client is essentially asking you to take some level of risk with them. Before agreeing to this kind of payment, be sure that you know the industry, can fully understand the finances of the company, and most of all trust the people involved. This approach is not recommended for newbies.

Negotiating your prices based on a percentage of sales generated by a client is similar to receiving equity. This is usually offered by consultants whose services directly impact sales. You may offer, for example, sales or customer service training and the end user of your services are the people who generate or directly influence the income potential for the business. I would only recommend this kind of pricing strategy after you have been in business for many years and have developed a strong track record of measurable results.

Deferred income means you receive a portion of the total amount upfront and the balance is due sometime in the future. That could be months or years and is generally used when you are commanding exceptionally large fees for services. A consultant may do this to distribute her income over a few fiscal years in order to lessen a tax burden. Again, this is not recommended for new consultants.

Pricing is an Evolving Dance

It's all about how you frame it! Pricing is one of the trickiest aspects involved in launching and growing your business. Pricing is a journey not a destination; it takes time and experience to find your sweet spot.

Getting clear about your service mix and target audience is crucial to discovering your best pricing. If you want to serve new American populations, for example, but they cannot afford your prices, you will need to adjust your pricing, your target audience, and/or your services. If you want to serve large corporations with big budgets but are not getting any new contracts after you raised your prices, based purely on your competition research, you may need to reexamine your prices or learn how to market the value of your services better. Maybe you want to help people aged 30 to 50 across a wide economic spectrum and some people can afford your services but some cannot. Again, you will need to amend your primary client, your services, or pricing.

Pricing, services and customers are linked in an eternal dance of which you are the choreographer, director and leader. This means you are in charge, and it means you have to stand behind your prices. Just using market research or your coach's advice is not enough. You have to be willing to publish your pricing in proposals and price sheets and then stand strong. If you don't believe you are worth it, neither will they.

In your first three to five years, you may feel like you are more of a dancer than a director. Use this time to experiment and take incremental steps. Learn the basic steps and add more to your repertoire over time.

When to Raise Your Rates

An important step sequence in the pricing dance is knowing when to raise prices. I use a few indicators as a guide. Firstly, if you are logging more than 25 client hours a week and struggling to pay yourself and your bills, it's time to review pricing. Secondly, when you feel resentful about the number of hours that you devote to a project or client in comparison to how much you are billing, look at pricing. Thirdly (and I have actually had this happen more than once) a client asks if you're charging enough; automatically raise your rates.

You can use the rate of inflation, some market research, years of experience, or your gut feeling when you consider your rate. Most importantly, get into the practice of annually reviewing your prices. You may decide not to raise prices in the middle of a recession, but you can still review, consider, and be intentional. Making this a routine means that you are less likely to suddenly raise your rates by 50% to make up for lost time.

There have been years when I reviewed pricing, raised my rates, promoted them, and then backed away from them. Six months later, it was a completely different story. It's a dance and you are leading it.

As you gain experience, your level of advisement increases in value. When you are less experienced, it may take you several hours to get to the heart of the matter and effect real change for a client. If you have been in the consulting orbit for more than 10 years, you can probably identify the root cause faster because you've seen the issue or challenge with previous clients.

Everyone thinks their problems are unique to their industry, age, size of company, or geographic location, but experienced consultants can see the patterns and often have solutions that have worked for other clients. If it used to take you five hours to accomplish in the first few years and now you see it within an hour, your rates should reflect this.

It used to take me five or six hours to write a resume, including meetings, formatting, and editing; now it takes an hour, even for complicated resumes. Since I no longer offer a stand-alone resume writing service, I have no qualms about charging a premium hourly rate to advise clients about their resumes. I can cover a lot of territory in an hour because I have seen a lot of resumes. My 30+ years means I can go deep fast and deliver high value.

When I expanded into corporate-level consulting, I had good instincts, but it took several pre-meetings to understand issues and propose viable solutions; now, I hear familiar complaints and have some ready-to-go options from which clients can select based on their budgets. I still customize materials and resources but can use the same core materials because I tend to help companies at similar levels of growth, and I understand the kinds of challenges companies face in those stages.

There are times when I am in the middle of writing a proposal that I decide to raise my rates. In the moment, it may have seemed quite arbitrary to a casual observer, but in reality, I was instinctively applying one or all of my indicators and they paid off.

Learn to keep your sense of humor while you dance with pricing and you will be fine.

Other Pricing Considerations

Once you have your hourly, daily, and project rates, you will need to translate them into proposals and price sheets for all the various aspects of your services. Just telling a client your daily rate is not useful, especially if there is any complexity to your services.

Consider bundling your services with some products or offering limited time special pricing. Reward frequent or big budget clients. Seek small ways to improve the quality of the information or the experience of your services. It's always better to under promise and over deliver.

> *If annual gross sales do not cover cost of doing business, including paying yourself, it's time to seriously reconsider your pricing!*

Using your basic hourly or daily rate, you can build proposals to meet your client's needs. Every proposal can start with simply listing all the items requested by the client with your regular pricing; then you review and adjust as needed.

Extras That Add Up

Beyond the professional services provided, consider items like preparation time, travel and mileage, materials, and other bits that cost you time and money.

Travel expenses (mileage, airfare, rental cars, meals, and lodging) can add considerable costs and they can be either an additional line item on an invoice or folded into a flat fee. General mileage is usually included in your pricing if the client site is within a reasonable commuting distance from your office. Since I am in Vermont and much of the state is rural, for example, I charge for mileage when I leave the county where I live. I use the rate set by the IRS to calculate what I charge for mileage and it is a separate line item on the invoice.

You can also charge for your travel time instead of miles traveled. I had an accountant who was glad to meet with me in my office if I was willing to pay her hourly consulting rate for the time it took her to travel. At the time, her hourly rate was about the same as mine, so I chose to meet at her office.

You can fold meals and lodging into daily rates, but only after you are an experienced consultant and understand the full costs associated with your time. Generally, consultants either charge a per diem that includes all meals and lodging, allowing them to manage their costs or they charge for actual costs. You may use either method, depending on how your client accounts for expenses.

Unless your client is paying for your airfare or delivering you to their site via a private jet or limo, you will generally charge actual costs for airfare. When your daily rate exceeds $10,000, however, you may consider folding travel into your fees.

An overlooked source of added value and revenue for consultants and trainers is fees for materials. While your materials may be several pages of paper that you printed or copied in your office, they have an intrinsic value beyond the paper. If you developed them, compiled them, or added value to them, it's called *intellectual property*. If you buy booklets or products and use them in your workshops, you will likely pass on the expenses to your clients, right? Why not do the same for materials you have created?

If your materials consist of printouts of your slides, however, I recommend that you fold the price into your daily rate. Be sure your materials fee does not exceed your daily rate or total for training. Remember that fellow who had a complaint about my materials fees after I sent the invoice? Part of the problem was that I under charged on my daily rate and the materials were nearly double the cost of the actual delivery of training. Lesson learned!

Bundled & Unbundled Services

Bundling encourages your clients to buy a large chunk of time or services at one time. Unbundled service offerings are the equivalent of an a la carte menu at a restaurant – each item is individually priced; bundled is like a prix fixe menu, one price pays for several courses.

Sliding Scales
Proceed with Caution

I have never offered sliding scale rates and I don't generally recommend it to anyone.

It is a common practice for new coaches or counselors to launch a practice using a sliding fee scale to establish a clientele. While you may want to help anyone and everyone, you will find that the majority of clients who ask for a sliding scale or who pay at the lowest range are not really committed to the process and are not even tertiary clients. They are more likely to move and cancel appointments, prematurely end services, or simply not make any progress.

Additionally, shifting from a sliding scale to a set fee may be logistically and relationally awkward. Telling a client who has been paying $20/hour on a sliding scale that your new set rates are $50/hour rarely goes well.

I know Solopreneurs who offer a sliding scale and swear by it. I have never seen their financials so do not know how well it really works. I believe asking a customer to decide what to pay places everyone into a very awkward relationship.

It's really better for everyone if YOU establish the value of your time and tell potential clients what to expect.

You can always change your prices and make exceptions. Remember you are the choreographer, and you get to call the shots.

As a coach, for example, you may charge $150 an hour for a single hour of time and offer a bulk discount of $14,00 for 10 hours for clients who want to dive deeper into your expertise.

If a client wants you to deliver a single workshop at their annual retreat, you may charge your regular daily rate. If they are using that workshop as a way to launch a program that includes more training, coaching, and consulting with the executive team, then you may give a discount on your hourly rate for coaching or include a monthly meeting with the leadership team as part of the package.

For daily and flat fee rates, consider bundling pre and post client meetings, mileage, and materials into your daily rate. You are more likely to schedule a post-training meeting with a client if they have already paid for it.

When bundling materials with services, be sure to tell the client the value of the materials in your proposal and invoice.

Charge for Proprietary Information

What's the difference between making a few copies for a workshop and proprietary intellectual information? Money!

If you are a trainer and provide handouts beyond a copy of your slides, you are leaving money on the table if you are not charging for materials.

When a client offers to print the materials for a workshop to save some money, I always say, "No, thank you". (Non-profits, schools, and government agencies are notorious for this.) Then I explain that the materials fee I charge is NOT for copies; it is for the proprietary intellectual information contained on those copied pieces of paper.

Before I was knowledgeable and confident enough to create my own materials, I bought materials from other experts and used them in workshops. I never had a client ask to purchase one booklet and make copies for everyone to save money. They always understood that those materials were proprietary intellectual property and that there would be a fee to use them.

No one would try to buy a painting from an artist for the cost of the paint and canvas – so why does anyone think it's ok to buy my words, knowledge, and useful information for the cost of making copies?

If you spend time developing your professional knowledge and skills by obtaining and maintaining certifications, attending conferences and workshops, or buying books, you are spending money. The knowledge and expertise you gain from all that expenditure influences the quality materials you provide. So, why not get paid for it?

One of the easiest ways to up level the professionalism of your workshops is to make a handout that accompanies your presentation. At minimum include the information from the slides and build in some blank space for notes and reflections. Look at the flow of the pages, think about how people will use the pages, and resist the temptation to cram everything onto a few pages.

Be sure to give proper credit to source materials, be honest about what you have "lifted," adapted, or created, and honor your professionalism by charging for your materials. Remember to add the copyright symbol (©), date, and your business name to your original materials, including your presentation slides.

Right from the start, I have strived to create quality handouts for workshops with a goal of eventually providing full-color, saddle stitched booklets. Before I could afford a fancy printer, I focused on the design and used colored paper where I could. If I really wanted to impress a client with the materials, I used a local print shop and included the cost in the materials fee.

When charging for materials, just be sure that your materials fee is never more than your fees for the workshop. I adjust the per person cost according to the number of people. For example, I may charge $40 each for 5-15 people; for 50 people, I may only charge $20 each for the same materials.

Upgrade Your Materials to Create Value

- *Create mini-workbooks or handouts that give more information than your slides*

Giving clients the "participant" version of the PowerPoint slides looks cheap and is rarely useful.

- *Print them in color.*
If you don't have a quality printer, lease or buy a higher-end second-hand printer that uses toner instead of ink. You will save money on supplies and outsourced printing.

- *Never let a client print the materials to save money.*
Reiterate that your materials are "intellectual property," not just "copies". Printing materials yourself also ensures quality control – remember they are part of your branding image.

- *Copyright your materials.*
Include your name, company name, date, email, and phone number so that if someone does make a copy of them or pass them along, your name is still attached.

Reward Primary Customers

Your primary customers purchase your services often and/or select your highest ticket items without dickering. Rewarding them for their loyalty and commitment is one way to keep them coming back for more.

Loyalty programs for regular customers are an easy form of reward. Just like a coffee shop that offers the 13th cup of coffee for free, coaches can offer a regular client one free appointment after a dozen. The free appointment can be packaged as "buy 10, get one free" or bundled into a package. Either way, the client gets a bonus for buying more.

If a corporate client books a year or more of training with you, consider either including materials or significantly discounting them. I have even included follow-up coaching as part of an extensive workshop series.

The main point is to make it worthwhile for your best customers to come back for more and bring their friends. Loyal customers are the backbone of your business.

Use Specials & Coupons Strategically

Introductory pricing, special deals, and coupons can be great ways to attract customers. However, consultative service providers rarely use these methods because they can cheapen the perceived value.

Some exceptions include offering members of a professional group a "member discount" as a professional courtesy; offering free or inexpensive workshops or webinars with a limited-time discounted offer for more services to build clientele; and offering non-profits a special discount.

Be careful not to discount too deeply because you may lose money and/or feel resentful about fulfilling on the offer. Specials and discounts are intended to generate sales, build a customer base, and infuse some quick cash into a business. Use them VERY INFREQUENTLY so potential clients don't wait for your next sale to enroll.

Avoid Clearance Sales

We tend to associate liquidation or clearance sales with retail stores when they are reducing stale inventory. This kind of promotion is intended to draw customers into a store where new inventory is conveniently displayed near the sale items. Loyal customers may receive early notice and entry to inventory reductions, resulting in deeper loyalty. Infrequent customers may only come for the sale events, but they are spending their money with you instead of a competitor.

Professional service-based businesses may use this method to fill open time in the calendar or empty seats in a workshop. Unused time is like stale inventory for service-based businesses. If you need to generate some quick income, offer last-minute deals or discounted programs that fill the spaces in your schedule. Just like specials and coupons this should be used as little as possible.

When a consultant uses pricing strategies too similar to retail stores, it erodes trust. If you offer special pricing regularly, then why would I ever pay your regular price or trust that your services are worth the regular price?

Pro Bono, Free, & Volunteering

There are plenty of non-profit organizations with valuable missions that I would l like to support, yet I cannot pay my bills if I give too much of my time.

If you want to give back and make a difference in your community, find a way to incorporate some pro bono service offerings along with some volunteering and free services while generating enough income.

To give you some perspective, Vermont has a wide variety of businesses and organizations with all levels of financial ability. The non-profit sector represents 20% of Vermont's economy and the State of Vermont is the largest employer. There are also numerous entrepreneurial businesses that employ between 10 to 30 people. In fact, 70% of the people who are employed in Vermont are employed by one of these smaller companies.

Non-profits nearly always expect special pricing and often decide to hire a consultant based on price. State agencies send out Requests For Proposals (RFPs) and the owners of private companies tend to do a little comparison shopping, although they rely heavily on referrals from colleagues and peers.

My primary customers are those small and growing businesses, but I also serve non-profits, local universities, and State agencies. I will say upfront that I do minimal business with the State because I find the RFP process tedious, remarkably time consuming, and rarely fruitful. And they don't pay well compared to corporate clients.

The one exception is the AmeriCorps organization in Vermont, aka SerVermont. AmeriCorps is technically a federally funded program, but it is administered by each state and has some unique qualities that allowed me to circumvent the RFP process in the beginning. Now that I am a preferred vendor, I do not have to jump through as many hoops to win RFPs. I offer a series of professional development workshops for members throughout their year of service, including workshops at their winter and spring conferences and individual coaching at the end of their service. I have been doing all of this at a greatly reduced rate since 2005.

I do this because I want to support the young people who give a year of service to the various non-profits around the state and help them launch their careers. Additionally, there were some lean times when AmeriCorps was my biggest client in terms of number of days booked in the year. They have been loyal to me, and I have been loyal to them.

This does not mean I offer the same rate to any non-profit that comes along. Not only can I not afford it, but most don't necessarily align with my core purpose as clearly as SerVermont does.

Since SerVermont is a government agency and they track all "in-kind" donations in order to calculate the full value of all the products and services received, I document the difference between what I charge them and the actual value. They categorize it as a donation; I call it Pro Bono services.

Pro bono usually refers to free legal services, but it literally means "for the public good." You do not have to give away services to incorporate the concept of pro bono into your pricing. You may reduce your rate "for the public good" as part of your socially responsible policy.

I also make a distinction between pro bono, free, and volunteering. Pro bono means I am providing my usual services to organizations that have approached me at a reduced rate or for free, depending on the circumstances.

Free is free. I may have a free offer, provide some free information on my website, publish something that I don't get paid for, or speak publicly somewhere for no remuneration. I usually consider anything I do for free to be marketing and evaluate requests for free services through the lens of my marketing strategy.

When I volunteer, I may be using my professional knowledge and skills in my role as a volunteer, but I am primarily serving the needs of the organization because I believe in their mission. I served on the Board for the Vermont Businesses for Social Responsibility (VBSR) for a decade. I chaired various committees, was a member of the Executive Committee, and chaired the Board for two years. I used many of my professional skills during this time to forward the mission of the organization. I also helped strengthen the corporate social responsibility community that I believe makes Vermont a better place in which to live and do business.

Setting a policy or guidelines for your business about when and how you will provide pro bono, in-kind, and free services will help you include some populations into your client mix that would otherwise not fit while also making a living.

Responding to RFPs
Proceed with Caution

I know many consultants who respond to every RFP that comes across their screen. I used to do the same. In the end, I spent a lot of time reading the details of the request, trying to suss out what price point would win the contract, and designing something that I was willing to offer for that price while meeting the specific criteria outlined in the RFP.

In 30 years, I have been awarded one RFP by the state of Vermont. It was even automatically renewed twice. I could only invoice for the workshop, however, if a state agency or department knew about it, had the budget, and made the request to schedule the workshop. I never booked a single session of that workshop because the training department never promoted it to the various state agencies.

State and local governments use RFPs because they are spending the taxpayer's money and they have to appear impartial or fair. But here's the dirty little secret about RFPs: if a State agency really wants a particular vendor to provide the service, they will write the RFP in such a way that only that vendor could meet the criteria. It's often rigged from the start!

The only other RFP I have been awarded was from SerVermont, and I was already a preferred vendor. The State was in the process of cleaning up their contracts and wanted all current and future vendors to go through the RFP process. As a preferred vendor, I knew the RFP was written to accommodate what I was already offering. And now, the contract is reviewed, updated, and renewed every few years.

4
How Can I Refine
My Pricing?

Breaking your prices down to the hourly, daily, and project level is a good place to start when formulating your services and projecting income. The moment you start offering a mix of services that are provided on an hourly, daily, and project basis it gets much more complicated to project your annual sales. To further refine your pricing strategy, let's look at pricing segmentation.

Your Pricing Influences What You Sell & Who is Buying

You've already been thinking about your preferred clients and services. These ideas, lists, and descriptions are works in progress and will continue to evolve as you grow with your business. Pricing segmentation will help further clarify who your primary clients are and what your primary service is, allowing you to provide a variety of services at different price points to enable you to serve people at varying levels of interest and commitment. It will also help you focus your marketing efforts.

Remember that defining your preferred clients and services is a layered process. Most Solopreneurs fumble and bumble for years through the process of clarifying exactly what they are selling and to whom they want to sell it. This is perfectly normal. Parts of this section may seem repetitive and even a bit tedious. It is intended to help you shift through the pile of possibilities and get to the heart of what you are embarking upon. Allow the process to guide you.

As you have already discovered, not all of your clients fit neatly into a single description. If you have been in business for a while, you have noticed that your clients can be widely varied. Prioritizing or segmenting your clients and services into primary, secondary, and tertiary levels will help you focus your resources and attention on what's most important. Your primary clients and services represent about 40 to 60% of your total sales. Your secondary clients and services represent about 30 to 40%, and your tertiary clients and services represent about 10 to 20% of your sales. Your service and customer segmentation inform and support your pricing and marketing strategies.

Generally, you will promote your best income generating service, aka primary service, to your best paying clientele, aka primary clients. You will not spend any direct marketing effort on your secondary or tertiary clients. Your secondary clients will learn about your services because they tend to aspire to be like your primary clients. Tertiary clients are usually referred to you by a client, colleague, or friend; they tend to be seeking an odd mix of requests and are generally people who fall outside of your primary and secondary client descriptions.

Services Redux

Applying the primary, secondary, and tertiary lens to your services will enable you to effectively promote your services.

There are many ways to create segments. If you are a coach, for example, a year-long program could be a primary service. But you could also offer three-month and six-month programs. These would not promise the same result, but maybe you could design a program around these shorter time periods. Not everyone needs, wants, or can afford a year-long program that requires them to meet twice a month with a coach. You could also create a series of pre-recorded messages that walk folks through a process at their own pace. You see, the same content or processes can be packaged in a variety of ways, opening your services to a wider range of people.

If you are a consultant and trainer, your 18-month organizational transformation program that includes executive coaching and customized training might be your primary service, but you may also offer different kinds of training such as one-day courses or a series of brown bag lunches through remote video sessions using Zoom, Google Meet or another product you prefer. Again, you would not promise the same level of results, but these could help you get in the door and will help fill in your billable hours. When you are wildly successful, you can turn down the one-offs and brown bag lunches because you don't have time in your schedule.

If you are a financial advisor, you may have visions of providing comprehensive financial consulting services for high-earning couples. But make room in your schedule for people who need shorter term advice or want to meet with you quarterly to review their investments on an hourly basis. These folks would not be your primary clients, but since they already have a relationship with you, they are more likely to level up to your full-service program when their needs change.

Remember, when I added hourly services, I didn't promote them. I always started by offering my 10-session program but not everyone needed or wanted that level of engagement. Some folks were in the middle of a negotiation and needed some quick advice. With ten years of experience, I had enough knowledge and confidence to ask a few key questions, get a quick read on the situation, and help people make a better-informed decision than they would have otherwise. And I filled a billable hour that was otherwise empty!

Let's start by taking a take a closer look at the services you plan to offer. First, list all the services you are considering and rank them from your most favorite to least favorite. Then add your prices based on the formulas in the previous section, ranking them from highest total to lowest total price.

Next, run the numbers. How many units of each of your higher-end services do you need to sell to meet your annual sales goals? If one of your favorite services didn't rank high in price per unit, you can still include it, but now you know it's value.

Warning! All you have so far is raw data. Now let's segment those services.

Your primary services are what you will promote first and foremost and are based on either historical or projected sales. This level should be all about your primary reason for being in business. If your numbers don't support that vision, take this opportunity to make some adjustments.

If your primary services represent about 50% of your sales, how many units would you need to sell to meet 50% of your annual sales goal?

Your secondary services naturally complement your primary business and are based on historical or projected sales. This level would generally feed into your primary segment. If you made any adjustments to your primary segment based on the numbers, consider moving them into your secondary segment. You may enjoy providing these services, but if the numbers don't support them, don't force the services for now.

If your secondary services represent about 30% of your sales, then how many units would you need to sell to meet 30% of your annual sales goal?

Your tertiary services include the odd bits that don't fit anywhere else. These are services you will provide but prefer not to (or maybe you just can't really charge much for them). Remember, this is your business and you don't have to provide any service just because someone asks for it. If you want to discourage demand, either don't mention the service or accept requests selectively.

If your tertiary services represent about 20% of your sales, then how many units would you need to sell to meet 20% of your annual sales goal?

Warning! Now you have more data, but there's more to pricing than data. Remember that pricing is a dance and it's more fun to dance with a partner. Let's take a look at how your clients fit into this process.

Clients Redux

Determining your primary, secondary, and tertiary clients is a bit more straightforward. Always start with your ideal client. It's likely that you designed your services around these folks, so who are they? Revisit your client description and go deeper. If, for example, you didn't include annual income as a descriptor, add it now. If your desired clients are corporations, use annual sales; if they are non-profits use annual budget. What are their habits? Why do they need your services?

Now write a slightly different version of your primary client. They may be in a lower income bracket, younger or older, or at a slightly different stage than your original primary clients. These folks are your secondary clients. If, for example, your primary clients are Fortune 100 corporations, your secondary might include any large corporation. If your primary clients are professionals earning more than $200,000 annually, your secondary could include professionals earning between $100,000 and $200,000.

Your tertiary clients are usually harder to describe. By definition they are undefined. Just remember that when someone contacts you who does not fit into your primary or secondary client description, they are automatically a tertiary client. After you have been in business for a while, you will be able to loosely describe them.

Reality check! Match your clients to your services. Will your primary clients be interested in your primary services? What about your secondary and tertiary? Adjust your descriptions where needed and run your numbers again.

Using the 50%, 30%, 20% ratios, how many clients at which level do you need to enroll? Do you need to make any adjustments to your pricing? Or your services?

If you have been in business for a few years, use your historical sales data and analyze your primary, secondary, and tertiary services and clients. Use your analysis to adjust your pricing, services, and client descriptions.

Remember, this is a dance, and you are in charge. There is no perfect pricing – your services, clients, and prices will evolve as you evolve. What seems too high right now will seem ridiculously low in a few years. Be kind to yourself, keep your sense of humor, and review your pricing strategy annually.

5
How Will I Get the Word Out?

Marketing and promoting your business can be as simple or complex as you want it to be. There are some basic elements like getting some business cards printed, creating a dedicated business email account, and having a solid elevator pitch. Depending on where your clients are in relation to your location, you will need to do more or less of an outreach online via a website or social media, and possibly an email campaign. Really, it's that simple for most consultative service providers.

You'll get a lot of advice to the contrary. People like to make marketing complicated (read *expensive*). Consider the source of that advice. If the person advising you makes their living by selling website development or marketing analytics or by managing social media campaigns, they are invested in creating just enough doubt in your mind to convince you that you "need to buy" whatever they are selling.

None of this is to say that a solid website, wonderful logo, and a strong social media presence are completely unnecessary. I just want to slow you down a bit. It's really easy to spend too much time, energy, and money on creating the perfect website, logo, and marketing strategy when you are starting.

It's common for new restaurants to have a "soft opening" before their grand opening event. No matter if it's a well-established franchise or a one-of-a-kind food truck, soft openings allow the staff to work out the kinks with a few customers before they try to deliver multiple hot meals to a packed house.

Consider launching a "soft opening" for your business. Use your network and current connections to enroll a few clients. Start small, beta test your courses and materials, and notice what works and what doesn't work. Make adjustments and keep moving.

In the meantime, develop your marketing strategy and fabulous website. Create and grow your social media presence. Write, build, create, and distribute whatever it is that you are promoting. Just don't try to do it all before getting a few clients and generating some income.

Remember, I started small. I was a subcontractor when I started writing resumes. It was my little intrapreneurial project – a resume writing service - under the umbrella of another company. I was entirely responsible for marketing my service, enrolling clients, and delivering the service. It was not my entire livelihood, and I knew I was building something bigger. From that base, I expanded into writing cover letters, job search coaching, and career planning. I didn't have it all figured out when I started and throughout the years I have spent a lot of time not having it all figured out. Be kind to yourself in this process.

Like pricing, marketing is a dance. If pricing is like an intimate Tango, marketing is more like contra dancing. There are more steps, partners, and combinations to learn, but it's just another dance.

Marketing & Promotional Plan

The primary purposes for marketing are to inform, persuade, and remind customers about the benefits and features of your services. It's all about capturing potential customers' attention and enticing them to buy from you. Having a marketing plan means you are directing all your good efforts to the right group of potential clients in a credible and memorable way. In other words, you need to create a persuasive communications campaign that attracts the hearts and minds of your primary client base. Start by focusing on the why and what of your marketing plan, not the how.

Let's dance with your potential clients. First you need to show up at the dance hall. Next, you ask someone to dance or you accept someone else's invitation. If you have just met, you need to introduce yourself, show them your moves, and discover if you are compatible dance partners. If they like your style and feel comfortable with you they will keep dancing with you. Some will stick around for one dance and others will dance the night away with you.

Showing up is the most important step. You have to be visible and present to attract the attention of your potential clients. If you are comfortable initiating connections, lean into that strength. If you are more of a wall flower, start small; ask friends to introduce you around, and keep breathing through the nerves.

The real magic happens the next time you arrive at the dance hall. Look for familiar faces, dance with a few favorites, and try a couple of new partners. You may not be the most graceful dancer or love every minute of it, but most things in life are like that. I am not a particularly graceful dancer. I am self-conscious about making a mistake. I overthink the steps, compare myself to more experienced dancers, and forget to breathe. Occasionally, all flows and I feel like the most graceful person in the room. Marketing is a lot like that.

For consultative professional service providers, the best method for attracting and engaging new clients is networking (aka showing up at the dance hall). If the word "networking" triggers uncomfortable sensations and embarrassing memories, then you may have some misconceptions about what networking is. Networking comes in many forms these days, including all forms of social media, and is the closest thing to "word of mouth" that you will find in a marketing plan. Learning the networking dance will transform your business.

If you are a human being who has lived on this planet for more than a dozen years, you have been networking your whole life. Every time you ask a friend for a restaurant, entertainment, or social activity recommendation, you are networking. Whenever you click on a link that you see on a friend's social media feed, you are networking. If someone compliments your haircut and asks who does your hair, you are networking. If a friend asks where you shop for groceries, you are networking. Networking is all about building trusting relationships, sharing useful information, and helping people solve their minor and major challenges.

The primary reason people freak out about networking as a form of marketing their services is because they think it's inauthentic. They equate strategic networking with manipulation. They think others will not trust their intentions. They think it's contrived.

Your recommendation of a restaurant to a friend is spontaneous and occurs in the natural flow of a conversation. When you promote your business, the conversation feels planned, deliberate, possibly opportunistic. But wait a minute! If you genuinely believe that your services can alleviate the pain and suffering of others, then why do you think you are taking advantage of anyone?

Trying anything for the first time is contrived! I would imagine that the first time you had a consensual sexual encounter it felt contrived. You were probably nervous, in your head, wondering what the heck your partner was doing at various moments, worrying if you were doing it right. I bet it was really awkward, too. So far, I haven't met anyone who didn't want to try it again.

After you have caught the attention of your primary audience, you will likely use the next most common marketing activity for consultative professional service providers: personal selling. This may be a face-to-face meeting with one other person, a "discovery call," or a formal presentation to a group. When you are in personal selling mode, you have the attention of your preferred audience, and you shift from informing and attracting to pitching your services to them. This is known as sales!

If the word *sales* sends you down the rabbit hole, take a moment and breathe in and out slowly. Pitching your services is a variation of the marketing and networking dance. You can learn the steps and with practice it gets easier.

Sales is not a dirty word. Sales is not about manipulation. Sales is about relationships. If you have the attention of your audience, they have asked you to dance again. Reframe your sales pitch from coercing an unwilling stranger into buying your "snake oil" into an opportunity to assist an interested potential client in understanding how your services can help them overcome whatever challenge they're facing. And if you are not the best fit for what they need, refer them to someone else. And there you go networking again.

Yes, there is more to a marketing plan than networking and personal selling. And yes, you will want a fabulous logo and website. But I want you to know that you can attract clients and generate sales without a logo and website. You don't even need a snazzy business name. You can simply get business cards printed with your name and email on them. If people trust you, they will do business with you.

Building trust is all about creating familiarity and being real with folks. It's likely that your personal story, including your professional experience, education, and challenges, are a big part of what motivated you to launch into being a Solopreneur. Another name for your story is your brand.

Before running out to get your business cards printed, take some time to understand your brand and marketing goals. Your brand is your story, including your "why." Reconnecting with why you want to offer the services you have selected to the people you have identified will help focus your energy as you build your business.

What is Your Story?

The good news is that you already have a story – it's the events and decisions that led you to this point. Simply put, your brand is the story that supports the central motivation for launching. It's the "why" of your business. The challenge is learning how to tell your story in such a way that you attract the attention of potential clients and keep them engaged in such a way that they hire you.

To start, let's take a moment to review the solutions you offer, your elevator pitch, and unique selling proposition.

Solutions

The solutions you offer to assist your clients in overcoming their obstacles are rooted in the why of your business. You see and experience a unique set of issues, challenges, and problems that individuals, groups, and companies experience that prevent them from attaining the level of success toward which they strive. This insight is likely the key motivating factor for launching your business.

I was motivated to offer career counseling services because I noticed that most people don't understand what they have to offer to employers, and they don't know how to tell their stories effectively. Their resumes are regurgitations of every job ever held; they apply for jobs that are a bad fit, and they experience the interview process as if it is an inquisition. As my business has grown, I have added other services in response to the challenges I observed in teams, leadership, and entrepreneurial development.

Elevator Pitch & Unique Selling Proposition

Unpacking your tidy little statements will give you some language. Look back through the exercise that helped you identify your USP to create your pitch. Refine your answers to who you are, what you offer, the main contributions you make, and what you want the listener to do after hearing your pitch.

Remember that other consultants offer similar or same-sounding services, but your motivation is unique. Did you spend many years in a leadership role within the corporate environment where you saw how these issues inhibited results? Did you have a personal overcoming and want to share your insights and solutions with others? Did you invent or discover a process, method, or tool based on your frustration with a repetitive issue? Get to the root of the root.

What is unique about your services may not be in the description of what you do; it may be in your approach, style, or the energy you bring. In my research with entrepreneurs of all kinds, I have discovered that there are clear patterns related to how people with different Personality Types tend to represent their services. The following may help you find some language, stimulate an idea, or bring more clarity to how you are unique:

Do you want to promote:
- *Your level of experience, your demonstrated expertise, and reliability of your tools.*
- *Your level of competency and focus on scope of vision for transforming the environment.*
- *The logical practicality of your service and how clearly it offers useful solutions.*
- *The innovative nature of what you offer.*
- *How your style, tools, and resources will help people create and maintain more harmonious relationships and thereby have better businesses, partnerships, and lives.*
- *How well you take care of the needs and interests of your customers.*
- *Your ability to apply theories in a process of discovery that supports clients in healing and overcoming their obstacles.*
- *Your ability to attend to the physical and health needs of clients.*

It's likely that two of these will resonate more clearly than the others. The idea here is not to include all of them – focus on what reflects your true nature. Think of these as dialects within the same language. I have learned to represent my services to many different audiences using a non-native dialect, but I didn't start there.

I started by focusing on my *style, tools, and resources that I thought would help people create and maintain more harmonious relationships and thereby have better businesses and lives.* I also leaned into my ability to help people create and act on *a vision for transforming their careers.* While I lean into the *process of discovery* and tend to *the needs and interests of my clients,* these are secondary.

Now that I have been in business for a while, it's fairly easy for me to talk about my *level of experience, demonstrated expertise, and reliability of my tools and the innovative nature of what I offer.* Again I don't lead with that.

Start with your strengths, focus on your people, and do what you do best. The rest will come in time.

Drafting the Basic Story Line:

- What was your role in creating and resolving the challenge? (creator, designer, implementor)
- What pivotal moment or series of events shifted your perspective?
- What actions did you take after that pivotal moment?
- What were the results?
- What have you done since then to improve the process, tools, and resources?

Now write five to ten sentences based on your answers. This version is what's called a "shitty rough draft." It will feel choppy and unfinished. If you like to talk out your ideas, practice telling your story to a few friends. If you prefer to think out your ideas, make a few more revisions, then practice by telling your story to your reflection in the mirror or reciting it into a recording device.

Notice how easily it flows. Do you get tongue tided? Is it wordy? Are you or the listener bored with your story before you finish? Keep refining, editing, experimenting. There will be a moment when you know you have it. Your story will naturally flow, you will be excited, your listener will be engaged, and they will want to know more.

Note: if you have more of a "think it through" style, there comes a point when you have to practice your story on real people. Select a few close and trusted friends or colleagues and let them know you are practicing. It may seem awkward, but it will help.

6
How Can I Network Like a Pro?

As you know already, I am an advocate for establishing and tapping into your network to generate sales. Since I have a preference for Extroversion (aka getting energized by interacting with the outer world), networking often feels like a natural expression. I have also coached plenty of people with a preference for Introvertion (those who are energized from interacting with their internal world), in successfully developing and accessing their own professional network. If you only know three other people on the planet, you already have what it takes to build a network, really! Networking is the least expensive and most accessible form of marketing available to consultative service providers. Simply, put networking is about making connections with other people, one person at a time.

Building a referral network is a natural evolution to having a professional network. A well-developed and tended referral network will feed you qualified leads for years, thereby reducing the need for most other forms of marketing. When a potential client is referred to you, they are less likely to be shopping around, will likely sign a contract more quickly, and are more likely to refer you to other qualified clients. The end result is less time marketing, prospecting, and negotiating, and more time delivering services to your people.

Expanding Your Idea of Networking

Before diving into how to create a dynamic referral network that will feed you for years to come, let's start by expanding your idea of networking. To the casual observer, networking looks like a game of "grip & grin," or shaking a lot of hands and exchanging a lot of business cards. That is one aspect of networking, but there is so much more.

First let's look at the who of networking. There are three main categories of people who will populate your basic network: Professional Peer Groups, Community Engagement Groups, and Networking Groups. Each of these offers different ways for you to meet and engage with people, demonstrate your unique approach, knowledge, and skills, and build your reputation.

Dynamic Referral Network

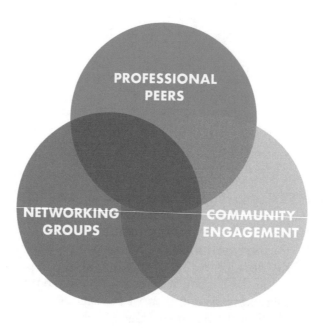

Professional Peer Groups

These groups consist of current, former, and future co-workers, local, national, and international colleagues that you meet at conferences or as part of your regular work, and participation or membership in a profession-specific organization. Every profession has at least one professional membership group.

- You know you are among professional peers when you can "talk shop" and others understand the references. All industries and professions have their own lingo and references, and your peers will likely speak your language.
- Professional Peer Groups are a resource group. You can be a resource to others and ask others to be a resource to you. You can become better known among peers when you assume ad hoc or regular leadership positions in your field, both paid and volunteer, and attend monthly meetings at regional and national conferences related to your field.
- Being known and respected by your peers is one of the highest levels of referral available.

Community Engagement Groups

When you participate in any organization such as a non-profit, municipality, or school or service groups such as Rotary, Lions Clubs, and Oddfellows, and you give of your time and resources, you build your visibility. You may serve on a board or committee for a non-profit, participate at a local school event, or be a community member on a town committee. These roles are all about giving your time, energy, and knowledge without any direct remuneration.

- When you are engaged in any form of community service, you are among people who share your values.
- Community engagement enhances your network by broadening your exposure while participating in activities that are meaningful to you.
- Select activities that genuinely interest you and align with your values. Then show up consistently and reliably. If you can't meet your commitments, be responsible for communicating your regrets well in advance. And most importantly, only agree to roles and activities that you are really committed to, otherwise you will likely appear as less than professional.

Networking Groups

These are general membership organizations like corporate social responsibility groups (CSR), chambers of commerce, young professionals, women's professional groups, women's business owners groups, social networking groups (LinkedIn, Facebook, Twitter, Instagram) or other groups where broad cross sections of professionals interact with the primary focus of mingling and networking. Formalized referral groups like Business Network International (BNI) and LeTip can also be included here.

- You know you are in the midst of a networking group when you are surrounded by a wide variety of people at various levels from a broad spectrum of organizations and industries.
- Broad networking groups enhance your network by further expanding your exposure. Start by selecting groups consisting of people you want to meet like potential customers, employers, employees, mentors, referral sources, etc.
- You may need to shop around and try a few different groups until you find the group(s) that suit your style. When trying on a group, attend several events before you decide it is or is not a fit for you.

Remember, this is a dance. If you are a beginner, don't enter the high-stakes dance contest. Start where you are most comfortable, learn the basic steps, and keep practicing. If you already have a solid professional network, trust your improvisation skills, and try a few new steps. Seek out the folks whom you respect or have known the longest, meet with them, and bring them up to date about what you are doing now. Be curious about what they are doing and what their next steps are. Have a conversation as peers and listen for common interests, goals, and connections. Ask them who they recommend you connect with to expand your network. Let them know how you can be helpful to them.

Make time in your weekly schedule to meet with one to three people for these kinds of conversations. Plan to have lunch or coffee out, meet online, or talk on the phone at least once a week with each of these contacts. Whatever your preference is, make sure you maintain this as if your business depends on it – because it does!

Once you get more comfortable, try a new dance group. The professional peer and community engagement spheres tend to be the easiest to start with because they tend to become natural extensions of life. If volunteering seems like a big step, consider how you can engage at a level that works for you. If time or convenience is a barrier, try showing up once a month at a local organization that you want to support, or be part of the "day-of" team at an annual event in your community. It may not seem like a great way to network, but you never know who you are standing next to as you hold cups of water for marathon runners or walk dogs from a local shelter. After dipping your toe in, you may discover that you want to participate at a higher level. Whatever you do, talk to the people with whom you are participating. Be curious, listen for connections, and most of all, show up when you say you will and do whatever you promise to do.

The broader networking groups are usually the most challenging. As an employee, you may not have had a good reason to participate in these kinds of groups so when you transition into Solopreneurship, networking groups can feel overwhelming. The good news is that if you have broadened your professional network, you will likely already know people in these more general groups. As you chat with peers, ask them about the types of conferences and groups they participate in. When you hear the same organization mentioned by more than a few people, it's a good indicator that you would benefit from participating in it, too. If you feel uncomfortable attending alone, ask if you can tag along with someone who is already going.

The real magic of networking starts when you actively engage in at least two of these three spheres; being active in all three is ideal. When you intentionally and consistently engage in these different spheres, you will quickly notice that people you know from your professional peer group start showing up in your community engagement arena and people you meet in your general networking groups may already be part of your professional peer group. When you interact with someone in more than one sphere, you have a deeper connection, a more dynamic relationship, and more opportunity to ask for leads and contacts to build your referral network.

Maintaining equal levels of activity in all three is unrealistic, even for the best networking dancers. It is natural and normal to have more ease and comfort in one of these areas and some difficulty in another. Keeping some activity in each sphere makes it easier to get more involved when you need or want to.

And by the way, your family and friends are part of this process. They form a large circle around these three spheres and can be helpful when you are building your muscles. Sharing your Unique Selling Proposition (USP), elevator pitch, and other details is easier when you are talking to people who actually like you and want to see you succeed. Having just one person who believes in you can make all the difference.

No matter what level you are participating at, there are two consistent actions that will guarantee a rich and dynamic network. When you attend or participate in an event, reconnect with people you already know and expand into one or two new relationships. I call this **deepening** and **broadening**. If you deepen and broaden wherever you go, your network will organically expand.

Be Realistic About Your Time & Energy

If you are naturally Extraverted, you are more likely to find activity in multiple spheres to be energizing. Just be careful not to spread yourself too thin.

Meeting and mingling in groups may seem like they would easy for Extraverts, but that's not necessarily true. Some Extraverted Personality Types tend to find small talk and general mixing in groups taxing when conversations lack a clear purpose.

If you are naturally Introverted, the whole idea of maintaining activity in three spheres may feel overwhelming. Some Introverted Personality Types report that mingling in large groups is especially exhausting. Introverted types are usually more comfortable in one-to-one settings or in smaller groups of people they know well.

Developing your network is a process that is never complete. It's more important to develop high quality connections than a large quantity. Always respect your style while inching beyond your comfort zone.

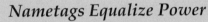

Nametags Equalize Power

Yes, name tags are awkward and never seem to be in the right place, but name tags are the great equalizers in a crowd. If we are both wearing nametags, then everyone has equal power in the conversation.

Walking around an event without a name tag gives you more power because you know my name and I don't know yours. Most people are not conscious of the power dynamic and are not completely aware of the imbalance, but it registers in the subconscious and can be off-putting.

As for where to put it, the best location, especially for anyone with breasts, is on your right shoulder. Using a lanyard means your name tag is either right on top of or right below your breast. This is a tragically unfortunate place to force people to look. Wearing it clipped to your waistband is even worse. Make it easy for people to see your name tag.

Placing it on your right shoulder means that when we shake hands, my eyes can easily move between your eyes and your name tag, conveniently reminding me of your name – and equalizing our shared power.

You can really juice things up by bringing your own custom name tag. Add your logo, name, and maybe your tag line. Print your first name larger than your last so others can read it easily. There are dozens of templates and resources online so have some fun with this and bring your personality (aka branding) into it.

Use the plastic name tag holders provided by the event organizers or bring your own. The best nametags, in my experience, have a clip or magnet instead of tape or a pin. They are easier to use and won't damage your clothing. The plastic "pocket" style provides an easy access pocket where you can keep your business cards.

Mixer Maximizers

- **Attitude is everything at a networking event!** Get your head around the idea that a mixer is all about developing, building, and deepening relationships. Go to a networking event with a party attitude and a party is what you will get. Go in thinking about who you can help, and you will find yourself helped along the way.
- **Dress Appropriately!** Be comfortable and be aware of the message your clothing is sending. If it is a gathering of mixed professionals, wear business clothing; if it is a gathering of peers, dress like your peer group.
- **Pockets!** Be sure what you wear has pockets for business cards; this is especially challenging for women. Leave bulky briefcases, bags, and pocketbooks in the car or at your table. If you don't have pockets, use your name tag holder as a place to keep your cards.
- **Do some research before walking in!** Which companies would you like to learn more about? Are there any particular people you want to meet who may be at the event? Who do you know that could make those introductions for you? You can often obtain a list of attendees prior to the event if you want time to strategize in advance.
- **Show up consistently!** To become known in a new group, you need to participate in 70 to 80% of its events. For example, if the group meets monthly, attend nine meetings in a year.
- **Deepen connections you already have with people you currently know.** This can be a nod across the room, a quick wave, or a brief conversation. Ask them to introduce you to other people at the event.
- **Broaden into one to three new connections at each event**. Read nametags and introduce yourself to people who work for organizations on your list of prospects, ask current associates to introduce you to someone new, find reasons to talk to people.
- **Use your elevator pitch!** Know what you want to say about what you do and deliver it effectively. REMEMBER: Benefits Sell, Features Tell
- **Schedule 1-to-1 meetings!** If you are talking to someone and want to have a more extensive conversation, schedule a time to meet within a couple of weeks of the event.
- **Find people interesting!** Remember that people like to talk about themselves, and most people don't feel seen or heard in their daily lives. But don't let anyone dominate your time. You are there to mix and mingle.
- **Practice effective listening!** Ask open ended questions, like "tell me more," use the four magic words: *oh, really, ok,* and *huh* with a neutral tone of voice to keep people talking.
- **Work the layers of networking!** Make referrals and connections to people in your natural network. Recognize that someone you want to meet may be two layers removed from you yet is still accessible.
- **Exchange business cards!** Write the date and event on the card. Make a note about your conversation on the card so you remember why you have that card when you discover it in at the bottom of your bag two weeks later.
- **Keep your business cards in your name tag holder or your pocket** so they are always easy to access.

Everyone Hates Me!

Even though I have a strong and dynamic network now, I still feel like I have two left feet in new environments. A few years ago, I was invited to speak at a conference in Syracuse, NY. A friend was supposed to accompany me, but she had to cancel at the last minute. I was flying solo in a foreign environment, and I was a little nervous.

A networking event for all the speakers and vendors was scheduled for the evening before the conference and I made sure to arrive on time at the hotel in order to participate. I was excited to mix and mingle with other speakers as a way to warm up to the crowd, but no one knew me in this group and I was feeling self-conscious.

Before entering the room, I repeated over and over to myself, "Stay away from the bar". I would be conducting two workshops the next day and needed to keep a clear mind. Upon entering the room, however, I was immediately disoriented. There was no registration table with name tags or even a conference representative greeting the guests. Within seconds of being in the room, I was belly up at the bar ordering a glass of wine.

Glass of wine in hand, I turned around and casually sidled up to a few women having a lively conversation. The woman closest to me did not shift her body to let me into the circle. I stood there for what felt like several minutes becoming increasingly anxious.

I was spiraling down, and every rejection and cruel playground taunt flooded my mind. "Who do you think you are anyway? No one wants you here." My mind chattered on. I could feel the whole group gossiping about me, jeering, snickering.

I nearly ran from the room. While I considered returning to my very safe and contained hotel room, I found a large plant in the corner of the lobby and took refuge. Hiding among the foliage, I had a good chat with myself. "You know how to do this; you are a good networker. Pull yourself together, woman!"

I went into the bathroom and took a good look in the mirror. I closed my eyes and breathed slowly in and out a few times. I almost dumped the wine but wasn't quite ready to let go of that security blanket.

When I returned to the room, I sidled up to another group of women and the woman standing closest to me opened the circle. I was in! A quick round of hellos and introductions and we were all chatting about our workshops. I had dinner with those lovely ladies and the next day had a few friendly faces in the crowd of 500 people.

All the rejection and awkwardness were in my head. I was the only one rejecting people; I was projecting my self-judgement onto everyone else in that room.

When I don't know what to do in an open networking situation now, I often walk out of the room into an open hallway or I go to the restroom. I take a break, breathe, and re-center. When I change my attitude and clear my head, the room opens and pretty soon I am in a conversation with someone and enjoying the experience.

Individual Networking Meetings

The big picture strategic networking is a process that can take years to establish and can be challenging to maintain for some. Depending on your skill and comfort level, you can use individual meetings to either deepen connections you make at larger events or start with a few one-to-one meetings and build up to larger group networking as you gain more confidence and skill. As with networking in groups, individual meetings can be easier when you see them as part of a system of networking rather than as a string of random events.

The people in your inner circle are likely friends, family, and professional peers. Select a few from this group who you know well and that you trust and respect. Let them know that you are launching or growing your business, practice your elevator pitch, share your bio and USP, describe your ideal customers, and generally get feedback about your business and elevator pitch. AND ask for referrals to people who may fit your customer profile, are in a collaborative business, or

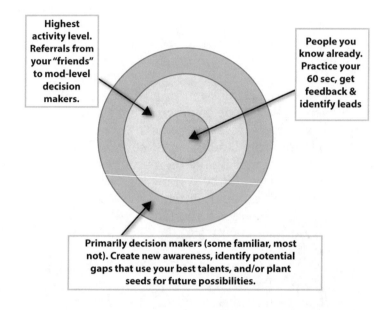

Highest activity level. Referrals from your "friends" to mod-level decision makers.

People you know already. Practice your 60 sec, get feedback & identify leads

Primarily decision makers (some familiar, most not). Create new awareness, identify potential gaps that use your best talents, and/or plant seeds for future possibilities.

may otherwise be helpful in your process. Get names, contact information, and reference your mutual friend when connecting.

There are three levels of individual contacts to consider: people you know right now and with whom you are comfortable, people you may know but with whom you are not comfortable making direct contact, and people who you don't know yet. As with any networking groups, start where you are most comfortable. This is usually a handful of people who are a mix of peers, friends, and family members.

You may know the people in the second ring but are not comfortable contacting them at this time. Your inner circle contacts can help make introductions or provide you with insight or information about them that will help you make direct contact. You will be the most active in the second ring. Be sure to ask for referrals to key decision-makers and other influential people in your community.

The people you don't yet know occupy your outer circle. If you have been refining your USP, elevator pitch, and customer profile in conversations with the first two levels, by the time you are meeting with outer ring contacts, you will be more comfortable, clear, and able to listen for pain points and gaps where your services can make a real difference. These folks are generally decision-makers and in a position to hire you, by the way. The primary focus in these meetings is to determine if your services offer viable solutions for their challenges, establish their level of interest and urgency, and move toward the proposal stage.

One-to-One Maximizers

- Meet in a convenient location and create connection. If you meet for lunch or coffee, pay for whatever they order.
- If you meet in your office, be a good host; offer at minimum a beverage like water, tea, or coffee. If you meet in their office, accept their hospitality. Even if you brought a water bottle or your own coffee, accept a glass of water at a minimum. Sharing food or drink builds trust and creates deeper connections.
- Ask questions that help people feel warm, appreciated, and important. Get to know people and leave a lasting positive impression.
- Get them talking and telling their story. Most people don't feel seen or heard.
- Use some of these questions to get the conversation started, but don't feel obligated to ask all of them.
- How did you get started in your line of business?
    (gives them an opportunity to tell their story and you an opportunity to listen for how you may be of assistance)
- What do you enjoy about the work you do?
    (helps bring positivity into the conversation)
- How do you distinguish your company in the marketplace?
    (gives them permission to boast and for you to learn their USP)
- What advice would you give to someone just starting in your business today?
    (highlights their wisdom and acknowledges their expertise, aka mentoring)
- What would you do today if you knew you wouldn't fail?
    (allows them to reconnect with their dreams and gets them thinking about new possibilities)
- What significant changes have you seen take place in your profession since you started?
    (allows them to reminisce about the good ole days and share more wisdom)
- What trends do you see coming in the next few years?
    (positions them as an expert in their industry; makes them feel important)
- What are some strange or funny incidents you've experienced in your business?
    (allows them to share "war stories" without being a bore)
- What have you found to be effective methods for promoting your business?
    (elicits positive reaction and lets you see how they think)
- If I were to describe your business to others, what are some key phrases or highlights you would want me to use?
    (allows them to compliment themselves and gives you tips on how to refer business to them in the future)

These questions were adapted from Endless Referrals by Bob Burg.

Extraverts Are the Best Networkers, Right?

I am aware that my preference for Extroversion helps me appear more comfortable in networking situations. I have, let's say, a "talent" for starting a conversation, but I still don't like small talk. I don't even really like having to tell people what I do for a living, either. I just want people to automatically know who I am and hire me. Sounds odd, right, since I am there to network and meet prospective clients? Even though I teach people how to create an elevator pitch about their business, I still resist saying mine. Everyone does!

For all of you who avoid open networking because you are sensitive, introverted, or don't like small talk, take a beat, breathe in and out and get over yourselves. You are not that special. More than half of the people attending any given event feel the same way as you do. And the other half have just learned to fake it until they make a connection.

Think of a few questions you'd like to be asked and ask others to respond to them. Avoid the obvious like, "So what do you do?" or "What do you do for fun?" or "How was your drive?" Is any of that really what you wanted to know?

Some of my favorites are "Which workshop did you attend in the last session? What was interesting about it for you?" or "What did you think about what the keynote speaker said when she …?"

If you don't want to dance solo, attend with a friend or colleague. Help each other meet people, but don't cling to each other. If you find yourself standing alone in the crowd, you can always join your companion and meet the person with whom they are chatting. Keep your nose out of your phone and your eyes on the crowd. It's likely that if you live in the area and have been a part of your community for more than five years, you will see someone you know. Everyone wears a name tag, so don't worry about forgetting names.

Whether you are meeting with one person or mingling in a group, talking to other people about your business can make you feel vulnerable or appear confrontational or intimidating. It may have been different when you were an employee because you had the shield of someone else's company to protect you. When you are representing yourself, your talents, your business, it can be scary as hell. Actively avoiding networking is a normal human tendency.

Yes, you can meet people via social media, but for professional service providers, there is no substitute for in-person networking. It's a vulnerable act to ask for help. People need to trust you before they will let you help them solve their problems. When people trust you, they will hire you and refer you to their friends. Mixing and mingling is the best way to become a trusted advisor.

So, make time to build your network and meet with people individually and in groups. Whatever method or approach you decide to use when developing your network, make it a habit. Try meeting with three people individually and attend a single event every month; join an organization and put their events on your calendar so that you attend at least 70% of them. Do the best you can; it gets easier the more you practice. I look forward to seeing you out there doing your best to connect with other people and promote your services.

Hate Networking? Join the Club!

If what I have said so far has you wanting to hide in the closet, take a moment and slowly breathe in and out. There are no shoulds here.

Well, maybe one, you should get accustomed to talking to people about what you do so they can decide if they want to hire you. Where, when, and to whom you talk is entirely up to you.

It is my experience, however, that a strong network is essential for any business owner, and particularly so for Solopreneurs who offer professional consultative services. The two most important aspects of developing and maintaining a network are to consistently stay engaged and to participate with people who are your ideal clients.

If you are overwhelmed by open networking mixers, start with some one-to-one meetings. If you like socializing with large groups, go forth and socialize. If you feel pulled in too many directions when you think about networking, start with the people you know in the environments where you are comfortable. For example, meet individually with a few trusted associates or friends. These may be people you've known for many years or just a few months. Make sure, however, that they trust and respect you and you trust and respect them.

Meet one-to-one for lunch or coffee if you are on a budget. Find out more about what different people do and let them know what you are doing. No matter what stage of development you are in, you can let people know your current state of affairs, inquiries, curiosities, and challenges. Remember, these are people who already trust and respect you, you don't have to work hard to impress them.

If you are in the infancy of describing your services, practice your elevator pitch and learn about what resonates or not. If you are seeking new customers, describe your ideal customer and ask your contacts who they may recommend. If you are developing a new program or product, test your idea and look for what can be improved, sharpened, or refocused. And be sure to provide the same kind of assistance in return.

Being a Solopreneur can be isolating and having a few trusted colleagues is vital to improving your ideas and sharpening your presentation. You may discover that the first three people are not the most amazing people you ever shared an idea with, but each time you practice your pitch, describe your customer, or talk through a new idea, you will become more comfortable with who you are and what you are offering.

Listen to where you stumble, hesitate, talk too much, repeat the same word, or phrase and make appropriate adjustments. And keep meeting with people for whom you have trust and respect. The next time you attend a larger event, find one person with whom you would want to have an extended conversation outside of that event. Get their contact information and follow up. Better yet, pull out your mobile device and schedule something before you both leave the conversation.

Once you are more established, these same people may be helpful in identifying new markets or opening a door to a key client. You may be able to refer business to them or help them select a logo or business name. The main objective here is to help others and be helped.

Just remember that while some people seem to work a room like a pro, hardly anyone likes idle chit chat. And the few people who seem to be effortlessly mingling are likely well known in that circle and are simply catching up with friends, colleagues, and clients (aka deepening and broadening with their established network).

> *Networking is all about making deposits into the community good will bank. The more deposits you make, the more you can withdraw.*

Building a Referral Network

The next level of networking is building a referral network. The most effective way for Solopreneurs in consultative service businesses to generate leads that result in quality contracts is to develop and maintain a reliable referral network. If you have already been developing your networking muscles, consider shifting your efforts toward an intentional referral network to fill your pipeline. Your current professional network is essential in this process.

Within your current network, some folks may consider you as a trusted advisor, others as a fellow colleague, and others as a professional peer. You may have more people in one area than another, but all you need is three people to start with and you can build an effective referral network.

Building a referral network and having a large network are two different things. With a large network, you will likely get business through word of mouth if you show up at events and meet with people one-to-one. A referral network, however, will greatly increase the quality of clients and projects that come to you and your potential clients are less likely to shop around for a solution.

A referral network is comprised of five to 20 people and can include former clients, influential people, complementary service providers, and people with whom you naturally affiliate. The essential criteria are that they know, trust, and respect you as a professional and you know, trust, and respect them.

Remember, if you know three people who you trust and respect, you have the start of a referral network. If you only know three people on the planet, you will need to expand your network (refer to the first half of this section). If you know thousands of people, you need to sort your contacts to find the gems. Start with the contacts you have now and shape them into your referral network.

Word of Mouth ≠ Referral Network!

Word of Mouth "advertising" happens when one of your customers or friends mentions your small business in a casual conversation. It's not intentional or planned. It's just something that they said in conversation

A referral network is a methodical process that you have put in place to capture qualified prospects through your association with other people. It's a system, and a system by its definition is a "process that produces predictable results." A system can be turned on and off at will, like a light switch.

Your business needs word of mouth advertising, but don't mistake that for the need to develop an intentional system for referral prospecting.

Become a Trusted Advisor

The best way to establish and grow a referral network is to become a trusted advisor among your peers, your current, potential, and former clients, and in your sphere of influence.

As you mix and mingle with other professionals, look for ways to help them problem solve, bounce ideas around, think things through, share concerns, and collaborate. Be sure to find some trusted advisors of your own, too. In the process, you will learn more about your field, and you will be able to demonstrate your knowledge and expertise. When people are comfortable exchanging their ideas and challenges with you, they are more likely to refer business to you or hire you directly, skipping the competitive bid process.

Be Prepared to Educate Your Referral Network

To prepare to meet with potential members of your referral network, practice and refine your (USP) and elevator pitch. Collect examples of projects and clients that represent your ideal service mix and client base. Select a half dozen individuals to start. Meet for lunch or tea to learn more about them, then share what you offer. Seek points of common interest and ask for their opinion or perspective on some aspect of your business.

Develop your network deliberately – this is not a casual affair. When you meet with people, interview them as prospective members. Get to know what kinds of referrals they are seeking. Ask them about the kinds of results they get with clients and get to know who their ideal clients are. Do they seem engaged when you share aspects of your business? Are you engaged when they share theirs? Do they ask good questions? Are they interested in learning more about what you do? Do you trust them? Do you respect them?

If you feel comfortable moving forward, ask them if they would like to be in a referral exchange with you. Please note, this is not a one-for-one exchange and you are not making promises about sending them work; you are creating an alliance with positive intentions and shared goodwill.

Before you leave, make sure you give them several of your business cards and ask for several of theirs. If you no longer carry business cards, make sure they have your contact information and are clear about how to make referrals.

Help Them Help You

Once you know someone wants to be in a referral relationship with you, help them help you find your next customer. Asking folks to "refer anyone they think may benefit from your services" is a waste of time. Off the top of their head, most people will not be able to make a quality referral.

People need a frame of reference to help them narrow the options from anyone to a specific person or company. Ask for an introduction to a specific person or type of organization. Reference a professional group you know they participate in and ask if there are other members who may benefit from your services. Describe your ideal or typical primary customer and ask if they know of any similar companies or individuals.

Provide them with typical scenarios or cues so that when they see and hear people use them your services and benefits will be triggered. Think about the kinds of questions your clients regularly ask or circumstances that result in them contacting you. What issues do you like to address? What challenges are you seeking? What are the types of problems in which you specialize?

For example, I help people who are in transition sort out what they are looking for and then help them take steps toward that future. I also help owner-operated companies that are dealing with growing pains.

These frames of reference allow them to "see" potential referrals in their mind. This may be limiting the number of potential people that your associates might know, but it is far more effective than asking them to sort through the ocean of people that they may know but can't recall in the moment. They are also more likely to remember your request because they visualized your services with much greater intensity.

> "You can get everything in life you want if you just help enough other people get what they want."
> -Zig Ziglar
> *famous sales trainer*

Show Them What You Do

Instead of just using demographics and psychographics to describe your ideal customers, consider telling a story that illustrates the pain points you alleviate, include several cues and common questions a client may ask when in need of the kind of remedy you provide. Your stories can be hypothetical if you are new in business or based on real projects if you have clients. The object is to help your contacts listen through your ears and see through your eyes. You want to be the first person they think of when they meet someone who needs the kind of services (or problem solving) you provide.

Stories are the best way to help people understand what kind of referral you are seeking. Remember what your English Composition teacher always said, "Show don't tell." I can tell people that I offer various kinds of workshops on Team, Leadership, and Personality Type along with coaching support and promise them that it makes a difference. But when I tell a story, they can experience them in full color.

I am particularly attracted to consulting with owner-operated companies that are facing the specific growth stages for 10 to 15 people and again from 20 to 50 people. The kinds of issues that arise in these stages involve the specialization of roles and loss of control by the founder.

My favorite corporate client is a software company that was on the verge of growing from 20 to 30 people. The owner, as well intended as he was, had been managing too many of the daily details for too long. It was time for him to develop a leadership team and focus on the larger strategic issues that would come with the pending growth.

Over the course of a couple of years, I brought everyone through a series of workshops about Personality Type, Team Development, and Leadership. I coached the owner and the people who were quickly becoming his leadership team. And I helped the owner identify the few people who needed to part ways with the company. Two of those people were what I call "problem children" and two were just burned out.

None of those departures came at the most convenient moments. One fellow, who was a subset of the "problem child" that I call the "Star Performer," was getting away with being a jerk. After I had completed several workshop sessions with the staff, he quit in an angry fit right before the company's largest trade show. He was the company's primary rainmaker and had quit at least three times previously in fits of rage. The next day, as usual, he apologized and asked for his job back.

When I coached the owner to stand firm and refuse, I didn't know what would come next. I simply asked him to trust the process. I knew that whatever would come was better than subjecting his entire staff to the verbal abuse that this fellow was famous for. In the void, several people stepped up and assumed his usual tasks and responsibilities. This process allowed people to shine in new ways and stretch into areas that had been off limits before. The staff finally came together as a true team. They had their most successful trade show ever and never looked back.

That company has 50 employees, is a world-wide leader in their industry, and is still going strong.

I use this example often, because it demonstrates all my services, brings my ideal client to life, and shows the value I bring to an organization. Additionally, in my market, there are hundreds of companies that fit this profile and I want to attract more clients like this.

Be Prepared to Ask for Referrals

To get referrals, you must ask for them. The biggest barriers to asking for referrals are fear of rejection or thinking that you are bothering people. While it's true you may be "bothering" your contacts, you are not "a bother". These folks are already your fans. They already trust, respect, and like you, remember?

You are giving people an opportunity to be heroic by recommending a qualified professional who can alleviate their pain and help them focus on what's important again.

> - *Only 10% of salespeople ask clients for referral, even though 90%+ of clients would be willing to provide them.*
> - *80%+ of B2B decision makers start the buying process by asking around for a referral from colleagues.*
> - *There is a 90%+ retention rate from referrals.*

Where to Find Referral Network Members

In addition to developing people in your professional peer, community engagement, and networking spheres to become members of your referral network, think about people you interact with in other arenas. Most of your referral network members are already part of your natural network. They are your clients, influential people in your community, and complementary service providers.

Look through your current and past client lists, identify influential people in your greater community, and seek out complementary service providers. You can even formalize your referral network into a leads group.

Some of these groups will be easier to access than others. You may not think you know any influential people right now, but you probably know someone who does.

If you feel awkward asking clients for help directly, you can at least provide quality customer service and let them know how much you enjoyed serving them. There is no obligation to build a formal referral network, but you can still use the information you gather while working with a client to increase your visibility and attract more clients.

Tapping Clients

Your current and former customers are likely to be the most enthusiastic about referring new business to you because they have already experienced your services. You are already a trusted advisor to them. Satisfied customers gladly tell their friends, family, and associates about how much of a difference your services made in their business or personal lives. It's a good business to provide the best quality service possible and it will only make it easier to ask for referrals, when the time comes.

Good customer service, however, doesn't always result in referrals. You have to be deliberate and proactive in creating referrals. Your best customers are ready and willing to give you referrals. You just need to ask for them!

Good Customer Relations Practices

- Ensure customer loyalty for life that result in higher quality referrals:
  - When a customer complains, do the right thing:
  - Resolve the issue; don't get defensive; thank them for bringing it to your attention.
- When a customer returns for more business, remember them:
  - People use what is familiar and they like to do business with companies who remember them. If you are not great at remembering names and faces, find some technique to help you get better at it such as a CRM database that allows you to retrieve customer information easily and quickly.
- When a customer thanks you for your services, say, "You're welcome:
  - Be gracious about accepting their gratitude and let them know it was a pleasure to serve them. Saying, "No problem," is dismissive and demeans the other person. Try saying, "It's my pleasure," instead.
- When a customer has suffered because of a mistake or misunderstanding, whether yours or theirs, make up for it:
  - Give the refund, pay for the overnight shipping, add something special, give a discount on the invoice. Consider it a marketing expense. When a customer needs a favor from you, do your best to help:
  - If you are not able or prefer not to grant the favor, help them find an appropriate resource. Remember, you want to become a valued advisor, so it's ok to advise them to use another resource.
- When you see your customer in public, be appropriate:
  - If you work with individuals or groups in a confidential environment, it's ok to say, "Hello." But don't reveal the nature of your relationship to others. If you don't immediately recognize them, apologize, and keep your sense of humor; this happens to everyone.
- When a customer brings you a referral, acknowledge it and say, "Thanks":
  - Create a system to track referrals and thank your customers in person or by sending a quick message; sending an email, text, instant message, or handwritten card are all fine.

Tapping Influential People

Influential members of your community are also excellent referral sources. These are the folks who seem to know everyone, remember names, and are able to talk to anyone. They may be public figures, owners of successful companies, heads of large non-profits, or real estate agents. What's most important is that they mix and mingle across multiple groups and tend to be good at reading people.

Identifying these centers of influence means looking more closely at your current contacts. Recall conversations you've had with them, people with whom they associate, organizations with which they are associated, and your general impressions or gut feelings. If you respect and trust them, it's likely they feel the same way about you.

Remember it is always best to start with people with whom you feel comfortable right now. You may not currently be connected to all the best networkers, but you probably already have people in your network who are more connected than you are at this moment.

Take a moment to think about who you know right now in any of the following categories:
- business acquaintances
- professional service providers

- business owners and leaders
- people you admire and respect
- family members
- close friends and acquaintances
- people you follow in the news or on social media

Build your network from the center out. As previously noted, use your inner circle to practice and build skill, confidence, and clarity. To expand your network, ask your inner circle contacts to help you meet and connect with other influential people and develop your middle circle of contacts. Use referrals from your middle ring to contact people in the outer ring. End every individual networking conversation by asking for referrals!

Once you have met with several people and have fully explored your second and third circles, start stratifying them into different levels in your referral network. Some contacts are naturally better at making referrals than others.

Keep track of who sent business to you and what kind of business they referred to you. Notice if someone sends several referrals that are bad fits. Bad fit may include clients who can't afford your services or clients who are not ready to act but who waste your time meeting about proposals that will languish. Other bad fits include people who may need a different solution than those you offer.

Don't Say Yes Just Because It's a Referral!

Just because the lead came as a referral, does not mean you have to run with it. You can always refer a referral to another consultant in your network. If this influential person repeatedly sends you inappropriate prospects, help them help you. Schedule a new time to further clarify the kinds of leads you are seeking. Keep in mind that you may not have been as clear as you imagined when you first met with that person or maybe your services have migrated into new territory.

Years ago, I received a few potentially lucrative recruiting referrals from a colleague, and I felt obligated to take them for two reasons. First they were referrals from someone I really respect and second, my schedule was a little light and I felt that I needed the business.

At one time, I provided recruiting services and while I didn't make a big deal about ending that service, I hadn't formally placed anyone in years when these referrals arrived. Within a month, that colleague referred two very juicy opportunities to fill two different executive level positions. After slogging through the recruiting process and finding good candidates, one company decided not to fill the position and the other seemed never to be satisfied. I was reminded of why I stopped providing recruiting services.

When the same gentleman referred another recruiting opportunity a few months later, I finally redirected him to two other recruiters in the area and reoriented him to my current focus. He was grateful for the referrals and grateful that I let him know what kind of clients I really wanted.

Another eager colleague was in the habit of referring companies that were not ready for my services. When she started working with a company, she could see that they had bigger issues than the very specific service she provided, so she would bring me in to meet with the decision-makers. These organizations agreed to meet because she was an enthusiastic advocate for my services. In the end, none of these meetings ever manifested into a contract. She tended to overrepresent what I could do and when I explained the process and level of commitment required to address the issues at hand, they all decided they had other priorities.

The best referral network members send you qualified leads who fit your ideal client profile; they send clients who are ready to act. Identify the strongest referral sources and focus your energy on nurturing relationships with the top 20%; this will net 80% of your referrals in the end.

Be an active referral source for others, as well. Stay open to the possibility that you are not the best solution for a potential client or that bringing in additional consultants for a specific project would be beneficial. Stay fresh with your network and you will be able to refer colleagues more effectively.

Accessing the power of a referral network will multiply your marketing efforts ten-fold. By engaging others in referring business to you, you transform your marketing resources from the efforts of one into the efforts of many.

Tapping Complementary Service Providers

Complementary Service Providers are people who are directly related in some way to your industry or profession, but who don't provide the same services that you do. These are the most powerful types of referrals because they don't directly compete with your services, but likely serve the same primary customer base.

For example, if you are an organizational development consultant, you may want to network with recruiters, outplacement consultants, internal corporate trainers, and other trainers who focus on different aspects of organizational development. Find the places where your services may fill a gap or pick up where their services leave off. A recruiter may know about big changes in leadership. Outplacement consultants may see high turnover and know there is a department in trouble while internal trainers may need an outside "voice" to communicate an important message. Other trainers may not specialize in your areas of expertise.

As with the other categories, you need to educate these complementary providers about your services. Help them be your eyes and ears in their circles of influence.

When I was ramping up my outplacement services, a mutual contact introduced me to a lawyer who specializes in Employment Law and was a big advocate of outplacement services. My niche in outplacement is to assist companies who are releasing one or two high level managers at a time instead of in large groups. The lawyer's clients were occasionally in need of releasing a single employee but were not accustomed to providing outplacement as part of a severance package. In a three-year period, he referred more than 15 clients to me, totaling more than $35,000 in business.

Tapping Your Extended Network

Beyond clients, key influential people, and complementary service providers, you have an extended network of people with whom you mix and mingle on a regular basis. They are your neighbors, friends, and family. They are all the people who you hire for services such as hair stylists, accountants, builders, plumbers, and coaches. They all tend to be in positions in which they interact with wide cross sections of people. Simply because they circulate with so many different people, they can be vital sources of referrals.

As with all the others, you need to educate them. Use the same initial approach that you used with everyone else: meet for coffee, give them your pitch, and teach them to listen to their clients with you in mind. List a few typical pain points that their clients may have, give some clues about what sorts of referrals are ideal, and leave them with a stack of your business cards.

Remember to get to know what kinds of referrals they are seeking, as well. Ask them about the kinds of results they get with clients, get to know who their ideal clients are, and leave with a stack of their business cards.

A Caution About Using Referral Fees

- Use them as an absolute last resort!
- Referral fees tend to muck things up. Money does not breed loyalty. Friendship, trust, and respect are what motivate your referral network to send clients to you.
- What can go wrong?
  - ✓The client discovers money changed hands and they distrust the quality of the referral.
  - ✓Someone claims they gave you a referral and you disagree.
  - ✓A direct competitor gives better referral fees, you increase your fee, and you have a war that no one will win.
  - ✓Good relationships go sour because of a referral fee dispute. A dispute breeds everything you don't want in a trusting relationship. Have a practice of generosity and keep an abundance mindset.

  There really is plenty of business to go around.

Join (or Start) a Referral Group

Referral or leads groups are generally closed groups comprised of professionals who serve a similar geographic area or have natural affiliations among other professional service providers. A group can be 10 or more people and meets at least monthly, sometimes weekly.

There are likely several established referral groups in your area. Some, like Business Network International (BNI) or LeTip, are part of larger international organizations; others are independent groups managed by the members of the group. All are intended for the members to share useful leads and information so that members of the group can grow their businesses.

If you choose to start your own group, select the 10 or 15 best of your influencers and complementary service providers and agree to support each other in generating leads and growing everyone's business. Meet monthly as a group, get to know each member individually, and learn together. Start with a manageable number of memebers and invite people as your needs evolve.

If you initiate the conversation, you will likely be leading the group, so show them your stuff and expand your network along the way.

I joined a local BNI chapter when I wanted to update and expand my referral network several years ago. I quickly realized that I could get more "airtime" in the meeting beyond my weekly 60-second introduction by volunteering to be the Education Coordinator. It was a great way to demonstrate my knowledge and expertise and simply have a bit more floor time during the meeting. Within a year, I was invited to be a member of the executive committee and when the chapter president left unexpectedly, I became the chapter president.

Remember that my business is all about helping individuals and groups get more of what they want from their time on the planet. So, while assuming the role of president was a bigger time commitment, it also gave me a perfect opportunity to demonstrate my abilities while helping other people build their businesses.

Part of the BNI system includes meeting one-on-one with each member of the chapter to better understand each other's businesses and more effectively make referrals. The regional director also coordinates regular skill-building educational opportunities for both the general membership and people in leadership roles. I thought I was a fairly good networker before joining BNI. I became an excellent networker as a result of my participation in the weekly meetings and additional training.

Explaining my services in order to receive quality referrals was my biggest challenge. Many of my fellow members were in businesses like real estate, insurance, and financial advising that were straightforward and simple to understand. Yes, a real estate agent does more than sell houses, but it's easy to understand that an agent is interested in people who want to buy or sell property. Consulting referrals are more nuanced. Representing the complexity of what I do in a weekly 60-second elevator pitch proved more challenging than I imagined.

I left the organization after two years due to a conflict with the previous owner of the franchise, but I am still in contact with several chapter members and we still refer clients to each other. Although I am not active with the local BNI group, I still refer people to the current owner because it's a powerful networking group.

BNI and LeTip require annual membership fees; some of the training is free, but not all. Both are for-profit organizations, and the regional director actually "owns" a territory, similar to owning a franchise. This is not to demean these organizations or discourage you from participating, but rather to help you make an informed decision about where and how you want to use your resources.

Tit for Tat is Bad for Business

You will find that some members of your referral network send you one lead for every dozen you send to them. It will feel unfair, and you will be tempted to stop referring business to them.

Keeping score between you and one other person is a very small perspective and will lead you down a lonely road in business. Instead, focus on the quality and overall number of referrals you receive from your entire network.

If you are not receiving enough or the right kind of referrals, you probably haven't developed your relationships enough or have been neglecting your network because you are busy satisfying your clients. Referral networks need maintenance. Schedule some one-to-one meetings, update folks on new projects, developments, and directions. Remind them of what you are looking for. Ask them about their business and make sure you are clear about what kind of clients they are seeking.

This is a long-term cycle. There is always someone new to add to your network because your business is constantly evolving. In addition, there is someone else who would like to add you to their network. Remember, no matter how many years you have been in business, there is always someone who knows more than you do and has contacts you need. You know more than someone else and have contacts they need, as well. Having a dynamic referral network is not an achievement, it's a life-long process that requires that you maintain an open-mindedness and a willingness to let go of any tit-for-tat thinking.

Referral Group Maximizers

- Be a leader in the group: Lead the meetings, as well as the membership, communications, or education programs. It's about demonstrating your strengths and getting a bit more airtime during the meeting while contributing you knowledge.
- Connect outside of meetings: Over time, meet with each member individually, learn how to refer to each other, become friends and trusted advisors to each other.
- Educate the members: Use all the tips discussed earlier. Help them help you get higher quality leads.
- Be generous and generative: Yes, track your results, but don't worry about how many referrals you have given vs how many received. If it's the right group for you, you'll get quality leads.
- Find people interesting: Listen more than you talk, seek areas of common ground, pay attention to what gives people joy, challenges them personally and professionally, and seek ways to help them achieve success.

Deepening Your Connection with Your Network

- **Sponsor networking socials, workshops, demonstrations.** Invite a cross section of influencers so they can mix and mingle. *Caution:* stay away from a heavy sales pitch, make sure the event forwards the businesses and/or lives of those who participate.
- **Newsletters and Blogs**
-      Keep the information relevant to the audience.
-      *Caution:* too much information risks overwhelming your membership, and they will start ignoring you. Don't take it
-      personally if someone unsubscribes.
- **Invite members of your network as a guest to relevant events.** Based on your knowledge of their interests and challenges, buy an extra ticket for a conference or event and pay for their dinner and drinks. *Caution:* this can be expensive. You need to balance what you can afford with the potetial payback. This is a marketing exspense.
- **Send them a useful gift**
-      Send relevant books, subscriptions, and other items that surface in
-      your conversations. Find an occasion beyond the winter holiday
-      season to send a card. Birthdays, Valentines, and July 4th are all
-      good times to say hello.
-      *Caution:* this can be expensive and unwanted. Go slowly with
-      this until you better understand the relationship.

Care and Feeding of Your Referral Network

Once you have established and educated the members of your referral network, you need to nurture these relationships or they will wither and die. This may sound like a lot of work, but think of it as a plant that needs regular watering, an occasional transplant to a larger pot, and some fertilizer to thrive.

When a person becomes a referral source, find ways to stay in touch. Being connected via social media and sending an electronic holiday card is not enough. When you see something that relates to your conversation or a shared interest, send it with a personal note, or just a postcard. It's good practice to meet a couple times a year in person and pay for their coffee or lunch.

When you follow up on a lead, mention the name of the person who referred you. The new person is more likely to respond because of a shared connection to the same person. This helps you begin from a position of mutual trust. Be sure to let your initial contact know what happened with the lead.

As you develop new services or products, keep your network informed. Make referrals to them. Be friendly when you see them in public. Ask about their business and thank them for any referrals they've sent.

There is no one size fits all solution to maintaining your referral network. It's all about creating several points of contact, being useful, and deepening the trust and respect you already have with your contacts.

If you don't have the time or are not inclined to develop long-term relationships with a wide variety of network contacts, then focus your energy on a few referral sources. Go deeper one person at a time and build your network at a pace that works for you.

Rather than focusing on the quantity, build and nurture quality relationships.

Decide to Network

Use every letter you write
Every conversation you have
Every meeting you attend
To express your fundamental beliefs and dreams
Affirm to others the vision of the world you want
Network through thought
Network through action
Network through love
Network through the spirit
You are the center of a network
You are the center of the world
You are a free, immensely powerful source
of life and goodness
Affirm it
Spread it
Radiate it
Think day and night about it
And you will see a miracle happen:
the Greatness of your own life
In a world of big powers, media, and monopolies
But of six billion individuals
Networking is the new freedom
the new democracy
A new form of happiness

Robert Muller (b. 1923, d. 2010)

Muller was an international civil servant with the United Nations. Serving with the UN for 40 years and rising to the rank of Assistant Secretary-General, his ideas about world government, world peace and spirituality led to the increased representation of religions in the UN, especially of New Age Movement. He was known by some as "the philosopher of the United Nations".

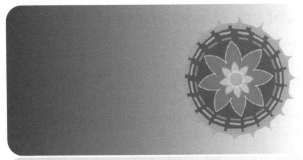

7
How Do I Create a Marketing Strategy?

Demystifying Marketing

"How do I design a website? Maybe a Facebook page is all I need. What about LinkedIn, Twitter, Instagram, or maybe I'll use that TikTok thing? Should I hire a digital marketing specialist or someone to generate leads for me?" Do any of these questions sound familiar?

These and questions like them are the kinds of barriers that stop good people from launching their businesses. Marketing is essential for any business, but many people had highly successful consulting businesses long before anyone Tweeted or Liked or Linked with anyone else. Facebook, Twitter, Instagram, TikTok and whatever new social media application that is being created right now are all ways to connect with and engage your audience in the hopes that some of them will become paying customers. None of these media platforms will make or break you. In fact, it is completely possible to have a very lucrative and successful consulting business without ever having a website, using Facebook, or implementing a multi-dimensional digital campaign.

If you know who your customers are, understand how your services benefit them, and have a clear purpose for why you are offering those services, you just need to get in front of your potential customers and make a connection that builds genuine trust. It really is that simple.

For people offering professional consultative and coaching services, the best way to connect is to demonstrate your wonderfulness in ways that are useful and that enable you to connect with the intended audience. Remember, to the general public, one consultant or coach sounds just like another.

Your elevator pitch, tag line, fabulous business name, or amazing website are not what makes that essential connection. People need to try before they buy. Think about the last time you bought a new expensive sauce, wine, jam, or even olive oil. You probably tasted it before purchasing it, right? Specialty food shops know that that tiny bottle of truffle jam that you can mix with the single sourced olive oil and drizzle over a perfectly ripe fig is a risky, albeit a low risk, purchase. This is why shop proprietors let you taste nearly anything on the shelf. The more you try, the more you tend to buy.

Your clients need to try your services before making the commitment. This happens one conversation, one conference presentation, one useful post, and one free online webinar at a time. People buy services from people, not from websites and tweets. People buy from people who understand their challenges and can help them create useful solutions.

Developing Your Marketing Plan

For any given challenge, obstacle, pain point, or difficult circumstance, your potential clients have several options for improving their situation. To help them believe in your specific solution, you have to get your message in front of them when and where they are. Since most promotions bounce, roll, and fall away, you will need a combination of promotional methods to effectively inform, persuade, and remind your primary audience to find solace in your solutions. Using a few, well considered approaches is always better than using a little bit of a lot of options. Focusing your attention puts your valuable resources to better use.

If you already know who your customers are, what you are selling, and maybe even have done some market research to find out where your clients turn for the kind of solutions you provide, then it's time to develop a strategy with a clear message, relevant objectives, and the right mix of activities to get your message out.

Remember, the dirty little secret about marketing is that about 50% of what you do is a so-called waste of time and resources, and there is no secret spell to cast that will reveal which 50% to cut. In all the years of planning, implementing, and managing simple and complex marketing plans to promote a new service, attract a new client-base, or pivot my business, I find that when I intentionally, actively promote my business, more business comes in. But it's not always from the direction I was expecting. When I focus on corporate clients, more individuals show up; when I launch a new book, more non-profits contact me; when I target individuals, more corporate clients come knocking. It doesn't make any sense yet, in the end, I continue to generate sales.

> ### Seven Touches
>
> Seven is a magic number in marketing. It generally takes seven "touches" before someone will engage with your company. These touches include social media postings, articles, public appearances, and targeted email campaigns. They are part of the journey of discovery and engagement you create for your potential clients.

The bottom line in marketing is get engaged and stay engaged; if you fall out of engagement, get re-engaged and new business will always flow in. Having a general marketing plan is useful and will help you to get engaged and stay engaged.

Remember, it's a dance!

Facets of a Marketing Plan

Each form of promotion has its own features and functions. They include personal selling, publicity, sponsorships, packaging, advertising, sales promotion, and direct response.

For consulting and service-based businesses, personal selling will likely be the highest ranked method of promotion and advertising will be the lowest. Different methods bring different opportunities and challenges. Generally speaking, those who are energized by interacting with the outer environment, the extraverts, tend to be more attracted to and have ease with face-to-face forms of promoting their businesses; those who are energized by reflecting on their inner environment, the introverts, are more likely to be attracted to behind-the-scenes methods.

Extraverts, for example, may be more comfortable attending networking events than developing a digital marketing plan. People who prefer Introversion, however, are just as effective at using one-on-one networking to develop a strong referral network. Some of the details will be different, but the fundamentals are the same.

In the process of learning each approach, you will likely be more naturally attracted to and skilled on one or two more than others. The objective is to create a marketing plan that you can and will use to attract clients, not one that you should do.

You will meet marketing professionals who insist you must do this or that in order to be successful. I know people who swear by a particular method such as Facebook or Instagram, but I have not used either much in promoting my business and I still have clients.

Let's take a look at each of these facets of a marketing plan in the context of promoting consultative professional services.

Personal Selling

Personal selling brings humanity to the selling process. Instead of relying on paid advertisements to inform, persuade, or remind potential customers, you or a representative of your company gets to spread the word. Because you will meet in real time (using in-person, phone, Zoom, FaceTime, Google Meet, or other direct communications tools), you can customize the message and emphasis to fit the audience.

For some people, the idea of meeting one-to-one with people they hardly know and having to think on their feet sounds dreadful. Even for skilled sales representatives, this can be difficult because instead of representing someone else's products or services, they are selling their own services. It's hard not to take rejection personally when representing yourself.

A key element in personal selling is development of a referral network that feeds you qualified leads. Having a referral from a mutual contact shifts the meeting from a cold call to a warm call. Cold calling is the worst use of your time and is a sure way to put some serious dents in your self-esteem.

Personal selling includes general networking, building a reliable referral network, making public presentations, responding to requests for proposals (RFPs), and scheduling meetings with potential clients, based on your research and existing connections.

Personal selling focuses on relationship building and making warm calls to potential clients. When an individual contacts me about coaching services, I immediately set up a time to speak on the phone. I ask a few key questions and listen more than talk. After getting a feel for their situation, I may ask another question or offer an insight about their situation. I do not hold back or wait until they are a paying customer before offering some confirmation or perspective on

> ### *Word of Mouth ≠ Marketing Plan*
>
> No matter what you hear, word of mouth is not a marketing plan. Businesses that attribute their growth to word of mouth are not telling the whole story. They may not be paying for advertising, but they are using a combination of the tried-and-true promotional methods.
>
> Those companies may have stumbled upon their promotional plan by chance, but if you ask them what they do on a regular basis to attract customers, you will discover some form of a plan under the seeming serendipity.
>
> Creating a vibrant and engaging social media campaign is not word of mouth either. It's called *networking* and it's one of the most tried and true methods for promoting a business.

their current approach, making a connection, offering a bit of useful information, or referencing another resource that can assist them.

Since at this point in my career, about 80% of my clients come from referrals, most are already inclined to hire me, but not all are not ready to commit on the spot. In that 30-minute discovery call, I'm not trying to close the sale and I no longer fret when I never hear from an interested person again. My intent is to connect and be useful. If I have done that, then they will either make an appointment in the next few days, or at the minimum, they will reference our conversation in the near future, thereby promoting me as a good resource who was useful in their process.

It's not an accident that most of my business comes from referrals these days. I have invested many years in developing a dynamic referral network and promoting my services using many of the basic building blocks of a marketing plan.

Promoting services to corporations is trickier, but not dissimilar. The best marketing a consultant can do is mix and mingle at conferences, industry events, association chapter meetings, and wherever else your potential clients gather in groups.

Start by finding the conferences, professional organizations, and groups that already bring the people you want as clients into groups and meetings. If your clients are international manufacturers, join the relevant local, national, and international associations and attend the conferences. If your clients are women entrepreneurs, join your local women's business organization. If there are no women-specific organizations, join a general business group or consider starting a membership organization to attract your ideal customers.

Then attend the events, including annual or semi-annual conferences and celebrations. I recommend that you participate in 70-80% of the events for a year before expecting any real return. While this may seem like a long-term investment, consider the level of investment you are expecting a client to make. People hire consultants they trust and feel comfortable with; it takes time to build trust.

Speaking or presenting workshops at conferences is the next level. You may want to be the keynote speaker, but don't start there. Research conferences in your area and find out what their vetting process is for speakers. Let them know you are available and would like to be included in the next proposal request. Conference organizers are looking for good presenters and they are not always easy to find.

Public Presentations

People like to try before they buy, and public presentations are an excellent way to demonstrate all your fabulousness. Saying that, "I help people create the lives and businesses they want," is not enough. Just like telling a story helps people relate to what you do, bringing them through a presentation, workshop, or exercises brings your services to life.

To become a keynote speaker, workshop presenter, or group facilitator, start by looking for associations and organizations whose members match your primary client description. Next contact whomever organizes the events and get the details about upcoming meetings and conferences. Make sure you get added to the email list for presenters so you can submit proposals for presentations and workshops.

When making your proposal, keep your audience's needs and concerns in mind. Design an experience that will give them useful tools, resources, and insights into their issues while demonstrating your skills and expertise in the subject matter. Keep clear of smarmy sales pitches. You'll only have about 60 to 90 minutes most of the time - your presentation only needs to be a morsel from your menu. The tastier the morsel, the more likely the audience members will want more.

If you are a trainer, public presentations are perfect opportunities to show your stuff. If you are a subject matter expert or thought leader in your industry, keynotes are a great way to speak into the ear of decision-makers in your industry. If you are a consultant, facilitating a panel comprised of success stories from your client roster in a concurrent session is a great way to demonstrate the kinds of results you produce with clients.

Public presentations are not for everyone, but if you have a predilection for standing in front of groups, look for how you can incorporate public speaking into your marketing strategy. And of course, if public speaking is not your strength, don't rush into it.

Conferences are Key

I know they're expensive. I know you hate mixing and mingling. I know you don't see any workshops on the agenda that interest you. I know. Conferences are a pain in the ass. And if you are not attending them regularly, you are missing one of the best opportunities to connect with business that is available to humanity.

Conference brochures and promotional information focus on the keynote speaker, workshops, vendors, and sponsors. The price of admission and the possible added expense of travel and lodging often make conferences feel inaccessible.

Conferences, however, are so much more than a bunch of workshops. They are opportunities to meet new people, deepen connections with people you already know, and have unexpected conversations with people who would normally not even give you a moment of their time.

In 2015, I learned my lesson about the importance of conferences. I was diligently finishing the first edition of my book, *Leadership Styles*, for a June deadline, and I opted out of every spring event. May is conference season in Vermont and I can attend up to six conferences in a five-week period. Autumn 2015, I had almost no corporate business contracts. You see, when I didn't show-up I was out of sight, out of mind. I doubled down that fall and the following spring and didn't miss a single event. I filled my calendar the following year.

Still don't believe me? Talk to anyone who was in business during 2020. When COVID-19 ran wild over the planet, every conference, convention, and professional gathering of more than three people was canceled through the end of the year. That included music festivals, international conferences, political conventions, and every professional conference and event that you can imagine. Yes, some were able to translate their agenda to an on-line platform and people signed up, but a lot was lost.

Screenwriters hoping to meet with a director or production company, graphic novelists who were going to launch their experimental project, political candidates planning to raise money, and countless vendors, consultants, and industry leaders did not talk to each other. While it may seem dramatic to compare a local business conference to Comic-Con, the impact is only a matter of scale.

At every event I attend, someone approaches me and says, "I was hoping you would be here," and proceeds to ask for my assistance with a project or my perspective on new product, invites me to speak, books an appointment, or connects with me in a meaningful way. I left an event recently having booked an all-time record of nine appointments for the upcoming weeks. As I was leaving that event, an acquaintance ran up to me and asked if I would stay just a moment longer to meet someone. He had been waiting all evening for a moment when I was alone to introduce me to someone, but I had been constantly engaged in an intense conversation throughout the event.

Collateral

Collateral is a vital part of incorporating your brand message into everything related to your company that your customers touch, smell, feel, hear, and see. The physical experience of your brand communicates who you are and who you think your customers are. Your collateral supports the branding story and gives customers an opportunity to hold a piece of your company in their hands, creating mutual ownership.

Creating a logo that communicates their brand story is where most people start. Your logo will be on business cards, social media hero images, office signage, labels on materials, and your tradeshow booth. Collateral even translates into the appearance of invoices, proposals, training materials, and any other printed or electronic document.

And you don't need an elaborate logo to be in business! My first logo was my business name in a fancy font. You can also change your logo whenever you desire. Your clients are not hiring your logo or your business name – they are hiring you. Don't get too hung up here.

More important than the perfect logo is your color scheme and the overall feeling you want to communicate. Start with colors that appeal to you and incorporate them into your website, printed materials, and your customized name tag. Details like fonts, colors, and images help potential clients know if you are the type of person who can assist them.

Personal Appearance

An aspect that most consultants overlook is their physical appearance. Whatever your body shape or physical condition, what you wear has a huge impact on how your clients perceive your level of expertise and professionalism. This includes how your clothing fits your body, the quality of the fabrics, and your personal grooming. None of this is to say that you must conform to any specific standard of beauty or fashion. You can wear whatever you like. Just make sure it supports rather than detracts from your image and brand.

Focus on quality over quantity. Finding your fashion style will help you invest in quality items that can be tailored to fit your body. It's worth the money and time to hire a professional image consultant to help you find your look. Knowing your color pallet and the styles and cuts that work with your current body can reflect your brand. Understanding how to care for your clothing so that it looks good even after you have hauled all your materials and supplies into the conference room

Naming your Business

Your business name can be as simple as your name. Really.

While its temping to create a business name that communicates all of your fabulousness, people will search for you by the type of service you provide or your personal name.

I recently changed the name of my business from Career Networks Inc. to MRG Inc. (aka Markey Read Group). Career Networks was a great name when I started 30 years ago. About 15 years later, I had outgrown it. I was offering more than career coaching services and the name did not translate well into corporate training.

The companies that hired me, were hiring me personally. They were usually referred to me or were people I knew from my network.

In the beginning, your business name feels very significant. Don't get hung up here. Use your initials, your name, or an abbreviation that is useful to you and move onto other more important issues.

means you can afford to invest in a professional wardrobe that will last for years.

When I was just starting and didn't have a lot of money, I hired an image consultant to help me. I was young and wanted to project a professional image, but really didn't know where to start. The process was so empowering. I stopped buying trendy colors and styles. I focused on a color palette that enhanced my skin and hair coloring, I bought a lot of second hand and sale rack items but paid attention to the quality of fabrics not the price. Before I could afford professional tailoring, I altered my clothes to fit better (those sewing skills finally paid off).

Every ten years or so I get an update. I have regularly hired a professional to help clean out my closet, take a fresh look at my current wardrobe and create a shopping list for a few strategic items. I still frequent resale shops and sale racks, but I am very selective about what I buy. My body, hair, and skin have changed throughout the years and I want to honor who I am rather than who I was.

Personal grooming includes getting regular haircuts and styling your hair so that it does not interfere with your ability to move, sit, stand, and otherwise interact with clients. If you have a regular stylist, ask for advice. My stylist is thrilled whenever I ask her for help – she is a hair artist and always has great ideas. Whatever hair style you choose, be sure it is something you can and want to maintain. Getting your hair to look good should not be the most complicated part of your day.

Publicity

Publicity includes all forms of non-paid media coverage and is intended to promote a positive image, foster goodwill, and enhance your brand with the intent of increasing visibility and familiarity. It's free and you can generate activity via social media and through print, and broadcast press.

Traditionally, press releases have been the most common way to get the attention of the press readership unless there is some other reason you have risen to notoriety. In today's world of social media, podcasts, and digital content, you can technically bypass traditional media to promote your message, but your audience is less likely to believe how wonderful you are if you are the only source of that information. Having someone else talk about your ability to produce results will build stronger credibility.

I have had a haphazard approach to formal publicity. Completely by chance, I have managed to be interviewed by reporters from a wide range of media outlets including the local television news, various local newspapers, *Glamour* magazine, and *Mademoiselle* magazine. I have also been interviewed on several podcasts and been a guest writer for various blogs. I did not pursue most of these opportunities, but responded quickly when they arose.

The magazine interviews were completely serendipitous. A reporter from *Glamour* contacted a professional colleague, Barbara Baron-Tieger, who had written a book about using Personality Type in career development and wanted to interview her about signs of professional burnout. Since she was not actually a career counselor, she referred the reporter to me. Incidentally, Barbara had just been to Vermont because I hired her to speak to the Vermont Career Counselors Association for an all-day event. I know she knew other career counselors, but I was at the top of her mind when the reporter asked her for a name of someone who would be able to talk about burnout.

The most important aspect of publicity is finding the places to put your message where your intended audience will see it. Social media is the best way to disseminate information quickly and at a low cost. But not all social media is equal.

The obvious social media platforms like Facebook, Instagram, Twitter, and LinkedIn are good places to start. First, understand your audience and research where they look for information and solutions to their challenges. Then research the industry standards for your type of services. Use the platform you are most comfortable with, use it well for a while, expand into other platforms slowly. Launching a multi-platform program is intimidating and exhausting. Use analytics tools to help you focus. When attracting individuals, you have one to three seconds to get and keep their attention on social media platforms.

The best advice I ever received about social media was to take it slowly. Focus on one platform and gain some comfort with it before adding others. I have focused more on LinkedIn because it was the easiest for me. I am far from an expert on social media, but what I do know is that when I engage with people on any platform, they engage with me.

Placing your blogs, vlogs, articles, and digital content on platforms like YouTube, LinkedIn, and paywall platforms like Medium, Patreon, and Elephant Journal, where readers are seeking a longer-form, is best for attracting businesses. Be sure to include links to this activity on your website.

To get the attention of traditional media, contact them directly via a press release with newsworthy information. You may be launching a new service, writing a book, making a technology breakthrough, been awarded a prestigious industry recognition, done some community good works, hired new employees, merged with, or acquired another business, or moved to a new location. Promoting yourself as an industry expert, if you have the credentials, is an excellent way to get cited in the press when related stories emerge.

When you are quoted, interviewed, or featured in any traditional press (printed, recorded, live, or virtual) feature it on your website. In the current environment of digital media, it's very easy to create a link to an article, video, or recording.

Sponsorships

Sponsorships are similar to advertising because in exchange for money, a company gets to control when and where their organization is promoted. Sponsorships are unique in that companies use them to support events (conferences, sports, music, marathons, festivals) and organizations (usually non-profits) with money, products, and services to associate their services with the kinds of events and causes that reflect their brand.

In exchange for financially supporting the event or cause, the company name and logo are featured in all the related promotions (press releases, brochures, programs, ads, banners, etc.) for the event or organization.

Sponsorships are a low-cost way for consultants to get in front of target customers. Knowing your customers' psychographics, especially their interests and values, can help you sift through the options. While you may want to support the local high school sports team, for example, it's not the best use of money unless your primary customers are the parents of team members.

Select one or two sponsorship opportunities, be a consistent and frequent supporter, and participate in the events. Consider underwriting on your local public broadcast station to create name recognition.

Your association with an organization usually reflects the values and interests of the owner and should also align with your primary client base. Sponsorships do not always have to be a perfect match to your primary customers' values, but they should never conflict with them.

Because of the ease of posting positive or negative comments about a company on social media, consumers today are more likely to spread negative news or launch a boycott if your brand associates with a cause that conflicts with their values.

Be careful of inauthentically associating with a cause-driven organization that makes your company look good but that you personally don't care about. The backlash is worse than your support of the wrong cause. People want to buy from people they trust. Use sponsorships to build trust.

Sponsorships can help enhance your image and reinforce your branding story. For example, I regularly sponsor the Vermont Businesses for Social Responsibility events and conferences because I am an advocate for corporate social responsibility (CSR). CSR organizational practices usually result in better working environments and higher quality opportunities for all types of professionals, and that's the kind of world I want to live in. The members of VBSR also happen to be one of my client sectors. Participating in their events is part of my networking strategy; financially supporting their events is part of my overall marketing strategy.

Direct Response

Direct response marketing is any direct communication you make to your client base with a personalized message, including SMS and email campaigns. They are intended to stimulate an immediate action or response from the recipient. Product based companies use this method for sales and special promotions. Coaches and trainers often use direct response campaigns to let potential clients "try before they buy." Offering a free online webinar, for example, with a time-limited special offer attached to it is a common way to engage with curious, but not yet committed target customers.

You can send very personalized, sophisticated messages to specialized pockets of your client base or broad-based announcements. These messages can be individually crafted and sent to one person or be part of a chain of emails that reflect what their specific interests are. For example, I send individual emails to prospects based on a mutual connection in which I ask for a meeting to discuss an opportunity. These are unique and only between me and the recipient. Or you can send broad-based announcements. I have various automated series of emails that are sent when someone downloads a lead magnet or registers for a webinar. I can customize these letters with a name, but they are essentially the same for everyone who registers. I have a very occasional newsletter that I send to everyone on my email list as well.

Building and maintaining your contacts is one of the most challenging aspects of direct response campaigns. You may collect information about your contacts from your website contact form or through your networking activities, but that information can be ephemeral. This is a big reason many people use social media. It's rare for someone to change their profile name or close their account. Facebook and LinkedIn groups tools to use to create a captive audience interested in your area of expertise.

The primary feature that distinguishes direct response marketing from other sale promotions is trackability. Every personalized message has a code or marker attached. If you are using an application like Mail Chimp or Constant Contact, you can track who opened, read, clicked through, or ignored your message. This kind of data enables you to further hone your messages and more clearly communicate with your desired audience. This can become a very sophisticated science of consumer behavior with lots of analytics, but you can still use direct response campaigns to engage with people without having a team of business analysts in the back room.

Sales Promotions

Sales promotions provide extra value or incentives to your client base to act. They are intended to induce immediate engagement by offering a limited-time opportunity to "buy now and buy more" while spending less. Sales promotions, also known as "calls to action," work well as part of direct message campaigns.

If your client base is primarily individuals, you can stimulate early registration or fill last-minute cancellations for live workshops or events. Offering related or introductory products to existing clients at a reduced or bundled rate can stimulate additional revenues.

If you are serving corporations, however, sales promotions are less effective. The decision-making cycle for businesses tends to be longer and more complex, ruling out quick action on time-sensitive promotions.

As I transitioned into more on-line activity and broadened my geographic reach, I strategically added sales promotions because it made sense. There are more opportunities to engage with Solopreneurs on-line and I needed to create more buzz about my services.

Be careful with sales promotions. Use them infrequently to avoid creating a dependence on specials. They can help generate some quick cash in slow months, but they are not a sustainable

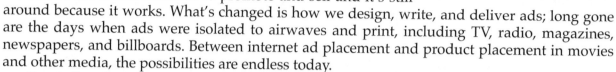

approach. While they are useful and abundant in our current environment, a better use of your resources is to build a clientele who values your services at the regular price. Focus on longer-term marketing strategies that build brand loyalty.

Advertising

Advertising is any form of communication about your company, service, products, or ideas for which you directly pay. It's one of the oldest methods to promote and sell and it's still around because it works. What's changed is how we design, write, and deliver ads; long gone are the days when ads were isolated to airwaves and print, including TV, radio, magazines, newspapers, and billboards. Between internet ad placement and product placement in movies and other media, the possibilities are endless today.

Generally, advertising creates one-way communication – from you to the consumer – resulting in minimal feedback. Knowing your target audience is key before launching any advertising campaign. Examples of placement options include ads on Google and Facebook, in print and on broadcast media, on your website or on other sites that charge to list your company or product.

Proceed carefully into an advertisement placement. Sales representatives are particularly good at making their medium sound like the perfect place for your business to spend money. Be wary of specials like one-time placement in special sections related to your industry, cold calls asking you to buy an ad on a local tourist map, and introductory pricing. Unless you already advertise in that publication with the special section, your customers are tourists, or you fully understand the long-term costs of an advertising campaign, these are all tricks that sales reps use to enroll you and they are all a big waste of money.

As with all the other methods of messaging, know your customer and your message. Use advertising as part of an overall strategy. You can burn through a lot of precious money in a poorly planned and executed foray into advertising.

I relied on advertising to start my resume service. It worked really well, too. I ran an in-column ad in the help-wanted section of the newspaper and people called. That was in 1992 before I even knew what a website was and I was offering a low-cost, focused service.

Advertising can be useful and sales representatives are really good at making it seem like a good use of your money. If you decide to use advertising, make sure it's part of a larger promotional strategy and not a one-off, spontaneous decision.

Your Marketing Plan

It can feel overwhelming to consider all these different facets of promotion, but with a little reflection you can create a simple plan that supports you and the growth of your business. Start with what you know and can afford. Get comfortable with it. Expand into something new and get comfortable with that.

As you know, I highly recommend networking and creating a reliable referral network. Instead of interacting with a lot of curious people who are looking for freebies, you will receive qualified leads and spend less time enrolling them. And they are likely to purchase your services at full price.

Marketing and promotion are highly experimental. Remember, half of what you do will be a waste of time and it's nearly impossible to know exactly which half. It takes time to understand what works, what is a waste of your time and money, and what needs to be hired out.

Before running around trying this and that in a desperate attempt to attract new clients, let's create some clear objectives and guidelines for your marketing plan.

Your Branding Story Redux

Your branding story is key to understanding and creating the central message in your marketing plan. When people connect to your story, they will respond to you. Review the rough draft of your brand story that you created previously and use these prompts to further develop and refine it. (Note: these questions are prompts and not all will apply to your story)

- What was the environment? What position did you hold before starting your business?
- What level of decision-maker were you in those circumstances?
- What did you like and not like about being at that level in those environments?
- What kinds of recurring issues, challenges, and problems arose that your position allowed you to address?
- What kinds of issues, challenges, and problems were you most drawn to resolve?
- What is your favorite part of resolving the challenges you like to address?
- When or how did you recognize the universality of this challenge?
- What kind of repeatable processes, resources, and tools did you create to respond to this challenge or to help people avoid it entirely?
- What kinds of results have you produced using these processes, resources, and tools and how many times have you produced them?
- What have you done since then to improve the processes, tools, and resources?
- What would other people who have participated in your processes say about you, your effectiveness, and the lasting results?
- Why or how is your approach better, different, more cost effective or efficient than how other people address the same issue?
- What key benefits do your services provide?

Now create your story, using any of the relevant bits from above. Your story is likely a composite of various stories. It's ok to use some poetic license when telling an illustrative or presenting a case study. You can combine some elements stories and nudge some of the details to tell a more succinct story. Use language, color, images, and sound to entice your target audience to engage in a conversation. Remember every good story has a heroine who rescues the situation. You are the heroine of this story.

Clarifying Your Objectives

Sending out well designed messages through multiple avenues will raise awareness of your services and products. But without some intentionality behind the activity, you will burn through a pile of cash quickly with little to no return on your investment. Take time to review and clarify your objectives.

What do you want in return for your efforts – awareness, higher sales, new customers, deeper relationships with current clients, introduction of a new product, or promotion of a special deal?

The Best Mix for Your Business

Finding the right mix of activities will maximize your efforts, save time and money, and allow you to focus on delivering those fabulous services you have worked so hard to create. Remember, it's not how much you do or

> ### Elements of a Good Story
> - Set the scene (recurring circumstance where the heroine uses her Superpowers)
> - Main action (what the heroine did when she discovered herself in this situation)
> - Main conflict (what challenges the heroine faced in "rescuing" the situation)
> - Resolution (result from the heroic actions the heroine brought to the situation)

spend that makes the difference. No one plans to fail, but many fail to plan adequately.

Having a strategy, instead of a string of interesting tactical tasks, provides a focus and timeline against which to measure your results.

Strategic vs Tactical Planning	
Defines primary objective and general actions to support objectives.	Defines implementation of specific activities aimed at achieving objectives.
Big picture focused.	Specific detail focused.
Long range: 1 to 5 years actions	Current and near future: weekly to quarterly activities.

Developing Your Strategy

Using your branding story and goals as guides, create a mix of activities that you think will inform, persuade, and remind your desired audience. Start by listing the individual tactics. Review the list and think about how each item supports other items to create an integrated plan. Then group the activities into the different promotional methods (personal selling, publicity, sponsorship, etc.). Take note of which categories have more individual activities; these are the primary facets of your promotional strategy.

Your mix will be unique to your business.

Allocating Resources

Allocating the resources to develop, implement, and maintain your strategy will ensure its sustainability. Your resources include time, money, and attention.

To start, draft a plan as though you have unlimited resources. Once you have your fantasy plan, look for what you can do yourself and what you may need help doing. Research your options to better understand which parts require your time and which parts require money. Unless you are currently a marketing professional, you will likely need some external help. Hiring the services of a professional can help generate sales more effectively than trying to do everything yourself.

Set realistic goals for your program and implement them to the best of your ability.

When hiring assistance, gather a few estimates from potential vendors and prioritize against your available funds. Be sure to stretch a little. Being too conservative could result in wasting money.

In the early stages, allow for mistakes and misjudgments. There is no science to this process; it's all about learning from experience. Expect to spend more money and time when launching and a lower rate of return. Be cautious of fancy sales pitches from vendors for websites, advertising, direct messages, and other promotions. It's their job to entice you to buy their services and it's your job to be a smart consumer and not swallow the hype.

How much you spend depends a lot on how much you can afford. I recommend that you focus on the "why" and the "what" of your marketing strategy. The "how" will become more obvious and feasible when you have decided what will serve your needs best. Do the best you can with what you have. Reflect and evaluate through the process.

Monitoring Your Results

Periodically check how effective your strategy is and adjust as needed. Keep in mind some parts of your strategy will have faster returns than others, so monitor each promotional method by the quality of the client and total number of sales per client you generate. Ask your clients,

"How did you hear about me?" and record what methods generate quality leads that turn into paying clients. Not all your activities need to have the same rate of return, but each one should contribute to the overall quarterly and annual sales goals. Advertising is by far the most difficult to measure.

Continually evaluate and update your promotional mix not only to correct ineffective promotional vehicles but also to adjust for growth.

Start With What You Have and Always Evaluate Your Results!

Many moons ago, after I had been in business for about five years, I felt like I had a good reputation and was well known in my community. I attended various conferences and events as part of my networking strategy and suffered through many ineffective keynote speakers and workshop presenters. More than once, I heard myself say, "I could do a better job than he does," or "I know more about this topic than this person seems to know." Then a colleague brought a conference brochure to my attention and said, "It seems like this is a topic that you could speak about. Why aren't you on the agenda?"

That year, I researched and collected information on all the events, conferences, and groups in the area, and before the Spring conference planning season started, I contacted each organization and asked to be included on its mailing list for proposals.

The following year, I did one to two events every month. Sometimes I presented a workshop or participated on a panel, and other times I had a booth. I accepted every invitation, even if I had to pay to participate. Some events were arduous and boring; others were interesting but too long, and a few were excellent.

At the end of the year, I reviewed each event and asked a few key questions: Did the event participants represent my primary clients? How many leads translated to sales? Were consumers buying my higher-level services or just wanting a resume? What did it cost me in terms of money, time, staffing, and energy to participate? Do I want to do it again? I honed the list of events to about eight that were worthwhile and headed into the next year with more focus. I still accepted the odd offer here and there, especially if there was a stipend for the speaker, but I was more discerning.

A few years later, a new event emerged that seemed to be exactly what I was seeking. It was a woman's expo and the organizer only allowed one of any kind of business to have a booth. There were even workshop timeslots available. I was a loyal participant for 10 years because the revenue I generated from new clients more than paid for my time and efforts. The reason I stopped relates to those questions I asked of the original set of events.

For the first several years, the event was held at a hotel conference center. This venue provided a professional feel to the gathering and attracted an audience in alignment with my ideal client. I always left that event with several strong leads that translated into paying clients. Additionally, I always presented a workshop in one of the coveted slots and had clients tell me for years afterwards that they first heard of me when participating in one of those workshops.

About seven years in, the organizer moved the venue to the local Exposition Center (aka the Fairgrounds) and everything changed. The building was a large open space with a concrete floor and high industrial ceilings. The noise level was almost deafening and I was in pain from standing on the hard concrete floor.

I would have overlooked all of that if the audience had stayed the same. But the fairgrounds attracted a different population - more families with young children and a lot of people looking for anything free. That first year in the new location, I went through almost half of my freebees within the first hour; people even took some of my table decorations and sample books. And no one stopped to chat. That was not my audience.

For the first two years in the new venue, I did manage to get enough good leads that transitioned to paying clients to justify the pain and hassle. The last year I participated was a complete bust. I was next to a booth that sold beauty products. The two young women running the booth attracted people to their booth by giving away hundreds of free samples. The crown at their booth blocked my booth completely. A few people stopped to talk, but they thought I was representing an employment agency or they just wanted to get a job at the hospital "for the benefits." Five people attended my workshop and at least two of them were there because their friend wanted to attend.

When I dragged my exhausted rear-end home that night, I promised myself that I would never participate in that event again. It was no longer worth the time and effort.

These days, I am still a regular presenter at six to eight conferences every year and my workshops are usually filled to capacity. While most events are within a two-hour drive, I also speak internationally and am invited to at least a couple regional events every year. Some events are great for a few years and then something changes. I still track relevant events and connect to new organizers every year. And I still evaluate events on those basic metrics I described earlier.

... and then the world changed . . .

When the entire world shifted to being entirely online in early 2020, I felt that I was at a great disadvantage. I had relied on in-person events for years and was good at navigating that space. I always left events with new appointments booked and a couple of prospects.

Overnight, everything transitioned to being remote and meetings were restricted to live or recorded video. My business nearly fell apart. I was not prepared to deliver interactive training via Zoom or network in such a limited space.

While I have had a website since 1994, it was a fairly static on-line billboard for my business. It was a way for people to find me, but not much more. And even with that mediocre website, people still hired me. I even tried my hand at a blog for a while. I was minimally active on social media, but I didn't like spending much time there. I posted occasionally, I commented less than occasionally, yet I maintained an extensive network of people. Social media was mostly an extension of my other networking activity.

I had intended to incorporate live and recorded video into my marketing and delivery, but I was too busy, uncomfortable with the medium, and mostly I felt no urgency to expand my skills.

Fortunately, I was not alone. Like others at that time, within a few weeks, I had successfully transitioned individual client appointments and group workshops onto Zoom and was still in business. By the end of the summer, I was fairly well versed in using recorded and live video and committed to expanding my skills. Then it was time to take a hard look at my business and reorganize how I provided services and what kind of services I really wanted to be offering.

The most important part, however, was that I stayed engaged with my core communities. I presented at and attended the few conferences that were able to quickly pivot, including an annual conference in the UK. I showed up in the "networking" rooms, sent direct messages to other participants in the workshops, and made appointments to meet via Zoom after the conference. I even managed to create a new networking group comprised solely of people who share my Personality Type. Quite organically, I and several other ENFJs formed a lovely cohort. We have been meeting monthly ever since. We talk about personality types, our experience of living as ENFJs and we network.

Because of my strong and active referral network I had plenty of business. I focused on what I could control, like serving my actual clients and expanding my on-line activity. I let go of the rest.

8
How do I Fill my Pipeline & Close the Deal?

Now that you know who your clients are, you've priced your services, started building your network, and the inquiries are rolling in, it's time to make the sale. Closing the deal and effectively negotiating contracts and agreements can make the difference between surviving and thriving as a Solopreneur.

Whether you are seeking individual, group, or corporate clients, you need to be able to close the deal before you can actually provide your services and generate income. The stronger your sales abilities are, the more billable time you will fill.

Unfortunately, the word "sales" has negative associations. If you thought networking was unpalatable, then "sales" is probably akin to having tea with the Grim Reaper. But without sales, there is no business.

Like networking, "sales" is another word for "relationship". Instead of dating, you are making a commitment; you are committing to providing quality services and your client is committing to being a willing participant in the process and paying your fees.

From Prospect to Contracts

While each client may be unique, all clients will move through several levels of relationship with you. In the beginning, they are likely part of your desired client base and network, but generally unknown to you. Next, they get referred directly to you or meet you in person and express an interest in knowing more. Once someone has expressed more than a passing interest in your services, they are now a potential client, and they have entered your "sales funnel". This hypothetical funnel is designed to help you move toward closing the sale.

Traditional sales lingo refers to the various levels in your funnel as suspects, prospects, active proposals, signed contracts, and scheduled projects. Upon expressing an interest in your services, a potential client becomes a "suspect," for example. When you have a discovery call or meeting to discuss how your services can help alleviate their specific pain points, they become a "prospect."

Depending on your pricing and the complexity of your services, a potential client can remain at the prospect level between an hour and several weeks. If you serve individuals and your services are fairly straightforward, you are likely to have a shorter sales cycle and move people to the scheduled projects level within 24 hours. If you provide organizational consulting to larger organizations that includes customized training and coaching, it could take weeks or months to schedule any paying work with a client.

Knowing your sales cycle, (how long it takes between the suspect and scheduled work phases) and your closing rate (the percentage of suspects who actually schedule work) are two key factors in filling your billable hours and building a sustainable business. Your sales cycle will help you anticipate workflow, and your closing rate will help you determine how many discovery calls you need to have every week to meet your weekly, monthly, quarterly, and yearly sales goals.

I recommend using a 25% closing rate to start. That means for every 20 suspects, you will successfully enroll five clients. Use your assumed average sales per client to estimate the number of potential clients, or suspects, you need to meet with if you close 25% of the time.

Sales cycles are trickier territory. To determine your average cycle, keep track of when a potential client initiates contact and how long it takes to close the deal. As a general rule, individuals will make decisions faster than organizations. As your sales skills and your referral network improve, this cycle will get shorter.

A large part of closing the deal is learning to be able to negotiate. No matter what size business you have, you will need to learn how to negotiate. To create income, purchase products and services, and manage your time, you will negotiate with all types of people. If the word *negotiation* makes you nervous, it's time to reframe negotiation from a competition with winners and losers to having clear, effective communications during which both parties get their needs met. It just may look different in the end than you expected.

Negotiating While Nervous

It's natural and normal to be nervous about negotiating. As a general rule, women are socialized to be conciliatory, compliant, and agreeable. As a result, they are more likely to cave when a potential client pushes back on pricing or questions their expertise.

Women are socialized to smile when someone stands inappropriately close, makes a sexually aggressive comment, or touches our bodies in an unwelcomed manner because we believe it will diffuse the potential for aggression. We are trained to be nice, polite, well-behaved girls, so as to avoid physical harm.

In negotiations, this translates to smiling and nodding while another person is talking, which is interpreted as agreement. As a result, women often give away too much while negotiating a contract for fear of losing an opportunity.

In the beginning, you will likely be nervous. You may never overcome being nervous. Being nervous is not an excuse for not trying or for stopping before you close the deal.

There is a little-known reward about being nervous or afraid and moving through your feelings. It's like leaping over a canyon. If you stay on the edge of the canyon worrying about the gap, you will be paralyzed. If you take the time to engineer and build a bridge, you are just stalling. When you step back, get a running start, and take your fear with you as you leap, you will pass through an invisible barrier and land on the other side as a changed person. The only way to develop your negotiating skills is to feel your fear and take the leap.

I am sure I have lost some contracts because the client thought my prices were too high or they didn't see the value I brought. But I know I have won contracts by standing firm on my pricing and proposals.

I had been in business for about 10 years when I received a call from a human resources director who wanted to discuss a potential outplacement contract. He was operating on a short deadline, as is typical with outplacement, and told me he was shopping around. When we met to discuss the details of my services and pricing structure, it became clear that this contract would be one of the largest I'd ever negotiated. He seemed impressed, but I could tell he wasn't ready to hire me.

He paused dramatically, took a sip of his coffee, looked me in the eye, and asked, "Why should I hire you?"

Every bone in my body felt like rubber and I thought I might slip out of my chair onto the floor. Instead, I took a sip of my coffee, looked him in the eye and answered, "Because I am the best." I did my best to smile confidently and maintain his gaze.

He smiled back and said, "Ok, how soon can you send me the materials I need to get things started?"

I was terrified throughout most of that conversation and when I got in my car to drive away, I started laughing hysterically. I still don't know what gave me the strength to tell him I was the best and then to hold his gaze.

That initial contract led to a lot more work with that company as they proceeded to lay off 20-30 people every quarter for six quarters in a row. It truly was the largest contract I had ever negotiated at that time, and I was nervous the whole time.

The first time I was hired to work with a growing company for more than a one-off workshop, I nearly lost my lunch on the conference table when the owner asked, "What other companies have you done this for?"

"Yours would be the first for me to take through the entire process," I said as calmly as possible. I added that I had successfully taken various non-corporate groups through the process I was proposing.

The next week I launched what would be a three-year relationship with the owner as he grew and developed his leadership team, added staff, relocated, and defeated a rival in a major legal battle. We are still friends today.

It's common to feel resentful for caving in a negotiation. It's a tricky balance to push back without sounding defensive. It may seem easier to acquiesce. If you agree to subpar pricing on a contract and feel unsettled, use it as fuel for next time. I didn't always look someone in the eye and tell them I was the best person for the job; I gave away too much for many years before I was able to speak up.

Understanding your value and pricing your services is the best defense against giving away too much or caving when feeling challenged. Do your competitive research, understand your market value, and create a pricing structure that ensures you can do better than survive on your income. No one will see the value you bring until you declare it.

The moment you start under-promising and over-delivering rather than underestimating and overdelivering you will be the respected and well-paid consultant you deserve to be.

Negotiating Contracts

Negotiating may sound like bargaining with clients, but when you use a consultative approach rather than a transactional approach to negotiating, it's more akin to deciding on a restaurant. If you are both hungry and agree to eat within the next hour, all you need to do is find a restaurant that meets the dietary needs of both parties.

Seek points of agreement and build from there. Paraphrase what you hear and relate stories and examples to show you understand their needs. Use a few key words or phrases, but don't parrot them. Watch for the moment of connection – it will sound like the laugh of recognition, look like relief, and feels like the wall crumbles between you and the client. When you make that connection, it's only a matter of time before you are doing business together.

Long gone are the days when the norm is that one party bends the other party's will in a no-holds barred wrestling match. If you encounter potential clients who try to assume a win/lose stance with you, let them find another company to fulfill their needs. There will always be clients with tight financial and time restrictions, but there is always room to negotiate the details.

The power dynamic is what tends to get in the way. If you are desperate for business as a consultant, you may acquiesce in negotiations too quickly (giving away your power) and agree to untenable conditions. If your schedule is full and you are overwhelmed, you risk being dismissive and driving a potential client away. No matter how full your schedule is, take the time to respond in a timely fashion and with as much thought as you can muster. Remember that your role as a consultant is that of a trusted advisor so no matter what title or size budget a potential client has, meet them as an equal and advise them.

Since you already know the value of your services, then focus on what you can provide within the given parameters. Just because a potential client asks you to lead a full-day team-building workshop for $250, does not mean that is what you will deliver. In the role of trusted advisor, identify pain points and clarify needs. Engage in a conversation to discover what kinds of results your client is seeking and explore options for delivery together. If they only have $250 to spend, look for what you are willing to give for that price or refer them to another consultant.

Ask directly about the number of people or units involved, timelines, and budgets. Most corporate clients have budgets, but often won't reveal the details. The common belief is that if they reveal that they have $20,000 to spend, you will size the proposal for $20,000 even if you normally would have charged less. Non-profits and smaller organizations are often upfront about budget restraints. They want your services but usually have small budgets for training; they want to maximize their dollars and don't want to waste their time with someone who is not willing to work within their limits. It's fine to say no and refer them to another company if you cannot meet their needs.

Finding the wiggle room in pricing is an art form. Generally, the larger the total amount of the invoice, the more room you have. For professional service providers, start with your established rates and then either include or charge additionally for extras such as pre and post meetings, materials used in training, preparation time, mileage, and other ancillary items. For example, if a client needs a training session for 10 people, charge your usual daily rate and include materials. Be sure to let them know you are giving them a discount. If you propose a flat fee for a project, for example, detail what it would have cost on an itemized basis in the proposal and on the invoice. You will emphasize the value of what you bring and let them know they got a deal.

Do your best to hold specifics about pricing until you have completed a few rounds of discussion. Create a written proposal and schedule times to review it together. Make changes based on the conversation and resubmit for review. If a potential client pushes for a price estimate, say you need more information before getting specific. You can reference how much it typically costs but wait to give details until you have agreed on what they really want. Remember, negotiating is a process, not an event. Stay engaged and let the process play out.

Similar to closing cycles, the more complex your services are, the more nuanced the negotiations can be. When I started, I made the classic mistake of pricing my services too low, but I had a high closing rate and easily filled my schedule. When I started tracking my hours more closely and recalculated my rates, I maintained a solid closing rate because I had the experience and a good reputation for quality.

I was reminded of this being a process when I recently met with a client to discuss a fairly complex contract for the fifth time. We had worked together about seven years prior when his company was transitioning from 20 to 30 people.

He was rapidly approaching 50 employees and needed more help. Since he knew me, I figured we would meet once or twice, discuss the details, and start the work within a couple of weeks. Nearly eight weeks later, we were still talking.

Each time we met, he asked more questions and wanted to discuss more options. This was a significant contract and I understood that my proposal was a significant investment in time and money, so I made accommodations. Each time I left a meeting, I was sure we had an agreement.

We blew past three proposed start dates, and I finally had to say that if we didn't start soon, I would not be able to deliver the series of on-line training sessions within his timeline. He had already scheduled an all-staff, in-person meeting before he contacted me, and I had other projects. At the last possible minute, he sent the signed agreement, and we launched within days.

In the end, it all went well, and everyone was pleased with the process. I was reminded that until the client signs the agreement, it's not a done deal.

Even though my current closing rate is about 80%, negotiating and closing the sale still takes time and attention. The process is more straightforward with an individual because they are usually the only decision-maker and the price point for my individual services is lower than for corporate services. This doesn't mean, however, that it's a casual expense for them. Spending your own money is different than making purchases from a corporate budget, so I never pressure anyone to close.

Because individuals usually contract with me for a discreet service that has a natural beginning and ending, I don't negotiate on price. I will negotiate payment schedules and the pacing of the service to support both my client's need for the services and my need to be paid for my time. The sales cycle for individual clients is usually about 12 hours and can take up to a week.

When an individual client clearly wants to enroll in a program but flinches at the price, I address it straight on. I ask, "Is this program financially feasible for you?" I emphasize that my services are an investment in their future. I say, "I teach people to fish for the rest of their lives instead of giving them a fish every week during the program."

If it's a matter of cash flow, I suggest breaking up the total amount into two or three payments. If a client needs smaller increments, I require one-third up front, as a show of commitment. Then we make an agreement for the remainder. I am not interested in breaking anyone's bank, I just want to be paid for my services by the time the we have our last appointment.

Notice that I don't ask, "Can you afford it?" or "What do you want to pay?" I help them overcome the obstacle without reducing my prices. It's a win-win.

Meeting the needs of corporate clients, however, is more complex. I have a variety workshops, materials, and other services that could potentially serve their needs. Depending on the number of people, the budget, and their level of commitment, an organization may agree to only a few workshops or embark on a three-year process with me.

Because of this variance, I don't jump into the pricing details until there is clarity about what they actually want. Before discussing the bottom line, I meet with the decision makers several times, provide outlines based on what we have discussed, and get a feel for their level of commitment and budget.

Only after we have agreed upon the general outline of services, do I discuss pricing. Numbers are often mentioned throughout the process. For example, they may ask for my daily rate or a general estimate before we discuss too many details. I am glad to discuss general numbers, but I resist getting too specific before I know the full scope of what they want.

Even after several meetings and review of potential scenarios, I know there is potential for more negotiations after I present a formal proposal with actual pricing. This process can feel arduous and tends to fuel my own insecurities about my prices and quality of my services. When a client is potentially going to spend thousands of dollars on my services, however, patience is always my friend.

Price is usually more significant in the mind of the seller than the buyer. It's important to remember that your fees are not the primary reason people will do business with you; nor are they the primary reason they will not do business with you. Aim to have your clients value what you do because you value and love what they do. If fees take center stage in your negotiations, it's your job to demonstrate how your services are unique. Your job is not to justify your prices, but rather educate your client about what distinguishes you from perceived competition. Escort them away from comparing apples to apples.

When compiling a final proposal, I estimate how many days and hours it will take for me to deliver the workshops and coaching; then I use a combination of my daily and hourly rate to price it out. If a client wants two workshops with 50 people in each and no follow up, I tend to price it on an "a la carte" basis, using my full daily rate; if a client wants 10 workshops with 15 people in each and coaching follow up, I look at the entire project and price it based at a "prix fix" level. I may reduce the materials fee, for example, or fold it into my daily rate, or I may structure the follow up coaching based on a flat rate, rather than billing on an hourly rate. The larger the contract, the more points of negotiation.

After all those meetings and discussions, it is rare for a potential client to push back. They may trim the project back, they may stretch it over two different fiscal years, they may break it into phases and commit to only the first phase to start. But you see, since I have established a relationship with them, they are likely to sign a contract.

Regarding the client I mentioned earlier, part of his challenge was that he wanted to agree to my initial proposal, but he was also navigating the costs and expense of flights and housing for his remote employees. In the end, we didn't do everything I proposed because he didn't have the budget. We trimmed a few bits and adjusted some logistics to maximize what I was willing to do within his budget.

I have had this process take from two weeks to three months. I have had clients agree to three workshops and then expand into a multi-year relationship. I have had clients start with the first phase and abruptly change course, negating the need for the other phases. I have had clients negotiate every detail of a proposal, and others who have scheduled work within a week of my first draft. Each client is different, and each negotiation is an opportunity for you to try something different.

Legal Contracts, Agreements, & Handshakes

The larger the total amount of the sale, the more likely it is that you will want a written agreement between you and the client. You may choose to draft a formal legal contract; you may create a written document that details delivery and payment schedules and requires signatures; you may use the final proposal as an agreement with or without signatures; and you may schedule work based on a handshake.

There are no laws, just guidelines and suggestions. I have used all of the above and none of them consistently. What is most important is that you and the client are clear about what, when, and how you are delivering your services, and what, when, and how they are paying you for those services. If your industry requires written contracts or agreements, use them; if not, use your discretion.

For example, I have drafted many written agreements to use with individuals and never them. I usually update a document after a difficult client experience. It's unusual to have an individual dispute our handshake agreement mid-stream, but it has happened enough times that I reconsider written agreements every few years.

I use varying forms of the final written proposal with corporate clients. About a decade ago, I did formalize my process and required signatures before scheduling, but there have been times when this was awkward. Some companies proactively request a contract and I always create one based on what we have already agreed. Once I have developed a relationship with a client, I use my instincts and their cues to guide the level of formality.

If there are a lot of moving parts, including travel, performance spaces, and guaranteed audience levels, I do recommend using written contracts. You have probably heard the example of celebrities demanding conditions like a large bowl of blue M&Ms candies in the dressing room. On the surface, this may seem like a prima dona's demand. But it provides a very quick way to check quality. If the bowl of blue M&Ms is missing, it means the client did not read the contract carefully, thereby putting you on alert to check the sound equipment, safety of the performance space, or time when your driver will pick you up from the hotel. Including very specific clauses in a contract can save you from dealing with other surprises that have larger consequences.

Finding your Negotiation Voice

Beyond contracts with clients, there are many opportunities to practice your negotiation skills. As you build your business, you will eventually hire contractors, such as a virtual assistant or video editor, and vendors such as a company that leases sophisticated printers. Finding your negotiation voice with clients, contractors, and vendors is essential.

The following tips will support your process of finding your negotiation voice:

- Start with an assumption of trust and respect.
- Build on what you can agree upon (every idea is at least 10% right).
- Listen more than speak.
- Account for the interests and perspectives of the other party.
- Use this knowledge to seek common ground and reframe issues.
- Anticipate objections and have ready responses.
- Practice and develop confidence in low-risk role-play or real-life circumstances.
- Understand what you want from the process.
- Know your bottom line and stick to it.
- Maintain an objective perspective, allowing you to overcome obstacles during the negotiating process.
- Know when to take a break.
- Know when to walk away.

Don't Bargain Over Positions		
Which Game Should you play?		Change the Game – Negotiate on the Merits
Soft Ball	**Hard Ball**	**Principled Negotiation**
Participants are friends	Participants are adversaries	Participants are problem-solvers
Goal: agreement	Goal: victory	Goal: create a wise outcome in an efficient and amicable manner
Make concessions to cultivate the relationship	Demand concessions as a condition of the relationship	Separate the people from the problem
Be soft on the people and the problem	Be hard on the people and the problem	Be soft on the people and hard on the problem
Trust others	Distrust others	Proceed independent of trust
Change position easily	Dig into your position	Focus on interests, not positions
Make offers	Make threats	Explore interests
Disclose your bottom line	Mislead as to your bottom line	Avoid having a bottom line
Accept one-sided losses to reach agreement	Demand one-sided gains as the price of agreement	Invent options for mutual gain
Search for the single answer: the one *they* will accept	Search for a single answer: the one *you* will accept.	Develop multiple options from which to choose and decide later
Insist on agreement	Insist on your position	Insist on using objective criteria
Try to avoid a contest of will	Try to win a contest of will	Try to reach a result based on standards independent of will.
Yield to pressure	Apply pressure	Reason and be open to reason; yield to principle, not pressure

9
How Do I Manage My Time and Energy?

Negotiating Beyond Contracts

Beyond negotiating pricing, contract details, and vendor contracts, you will have multiple opportunities to negotiate agreements. To start, you will constantly be negotiating the balance between making money, marketing, serving your community, and having a personal life.

A common myth about Solopreneurs is that since they "work from home" or "can work when they feel like it," that their time is more flexible than people who have "real jobs." This can lead to unreasonable expectations and demands on your time and attention. Learning to effectively say no to requests will help you keep the agreements that are important and minimize the number of shoulds, woulds, and coulds that can consume entire days when not managed well.

The first step is to only say yes when you really mean it. That is easier to say than do, so let's take a deeper look.

Think about the last time you agreed to something when you should have said no. Next ask yourself a few questions: Did you do it anyway and feel resentful about it? Or did you cancel at the last minute? Or did you do it cheerfully and then promise yourself you would never do it again?

If you keep your agreement, but do the task while filled with resentment, you will use twice the energy it would have taken if done with a cheerful attitude. And canceling at the last minute, unless you have a real emergency, is unprofessional.

The key to finding your true yes and true no is to keep every agreement you ever make. If you want to develop your ability to make agreements that really work for you, keep every agreement you make. It's the only way you will ever learn how to say "no." When you say yes because you don't want to offend someone, but then cancel at the last minute, you lose respect – respect for yourself and from others. Making excuses for cancelling takes a lot of energy and signals the people around you that you are unreliable. In the perception of your referral network, unreliability in one area can easily transfer to unreliability in other areas.

We also damage our integrity when we say yes when we mean no and when we say no when we mean yes. When you authentically and cheerfully fulfill your commitments, people notice.

I used to volunteer for nearly everything simply because I didn't give anyone else a chance to speak up. The moments of silence between a request for assistance being made and a person raising their hand used to feel excruciating to me. I didn't know that there were others sitting at the table who were just seconds from volunteering.

For people with a preference for extraversion, three to seven seconds of silence feels like minutes. People who prefer introversion, however, may need up to 10 seconds to consider the request and decide if they want to speak up. Now, I slowly count to ten. If no one steps forward *and* I actually want to volunteer, I gladly do so.

After keeping your agreement, pause for a moment to reflect. Then ask yourself: Was that a good use of my time? Was there an unexpected positive or negative outcome? Do I ever want to do that again? If so, why, and how soon or how often? If not, why, and what will I say or do in the future to that kind of request?

When making agreements in the future, ask more clarifying questions, listen for what the real request is, and then decide if you will commit. On face value, for example, the request could be for you to attend an hour-long meeting regarding elementary school education. When you dig deeper you discover the meeting is an hour's drive away, you'll need to peruse a 25-page report and prepare a PowerPoint summary, and you don't even have kids. You may be passionate about education, but is that meeting really the best use of your time and energy?

Apply this same kind of analysis to the community engagement activities that are part of your networking strategy. You may be highly committed to increasing access to education, but if you don't have kids or your clients are not the parents of school age kids, for example, consider finding another way to support education in your community.

Many moons ago, I met a fellow who worked for the Green Mountain Scouting organization. When he learned that I once worked in public relations for Boston University, he immediately recruited me to do PR for the Boy Scouts as a volunteer. I was so flattered to be asked that I didn't even think twice about making the commitment.

About two months into this role, I came to my senses and excused myself from it. It's not that I was opposed to Scouting or that I didn't think I could help. My stepsons had been active in the Scouts during their elementary school years but were in high school by then. I had indeed worked for BU in the public relations department, but I was there for less than a year and I was not that great at my job. Additionally, the gentleman who recruited me expected me to attend weekly meetings. I didn't want to spend my evenings at Scout meetings.

It was a bad fit all around; I was so relieved when I walked away.

None of this is to be intended to discourage you from helping a neighbor with meals after surgery, participating in protest rallies, or attending your 7-year-old niece's violin recital. If, however, in anticipation of fulfilling any of these requests, your feelings shift from joy to resentment, step back and ask yourself if they're a good use of your time and energy.

The best part of being more selective is that people respect your time more. I have a variety of interests, including raising more than 65% of my own food on my small homestead in addition to running my full-time business. As a result, I have an eclectic network and am asked to participate in a wide variety of organizations and activities.

Because I am thoughtful about which commitments I make, my friends and colleagues know I will follow through. Because I respectfully decline many wonderful opportunities, they also assume I am terribly busy. It's true that I am busy, but not necessarily in the ways they imagine. I have no end of projects, groups, and interests that can fill my time. I do not lack for ways to stay engaged. But I am intentional about how I use my time and energy.

How to Start Saying No

When you are sorting through requests for your time, start to plan ahead about how and when you will decline opportunities. Before your well-intended friend drags you to another protest rally, for example, decide where you want to focus your protest energy. Deciding ahead of time, reduces how often you feel caught off guard and gives you confidence and control over your choices.

No matter how enthusiastic she is, be friendly and firm with your no. Start by repeating the request, "You want me to drive you three hours to protest the use of digitally recorded music over live music streaming in the park?"

Be honest. Lying about your lack of concern about the use of digitally recorded music in parks will just lead to making up more lies to cover your story. Simply state, "That is not a hot button issue for me, and I don't want to drive three hours each way for that issue.

Speak for yourself. You're not responsible for everyone else's actions. Speak only about how you feel.

Discuss the possible consequences, "If I drive there and back today, I will not be able to enjoy my day off."

Separate the activity from the person. Let her know you care about her, but you do not wish to attend that protest rally, "You know I love spending time with you, however I don't feel compelled to attend that rally."

Suggest an alternative, "How about we take a hike this afternoon? Or maybe we can find a different rally to attend?"

If she persists, take a break from the conversation, "Hey, I have some other things I want to do today. Let me know if you want to spend some time together tomorrow."

Be prepared to accept the fact that she may not be happy with your decision.

How to Say No So That People Are Thrilled

Learning to say no and mean it is a great skill to develop; learning to say no and leaving the other person thrilled will transform your life. The key is being genuinely grateful for every request that crosses your path. That's right. Instead of experiencing requests as bothersome distractions, consider them as opportunities to be of service. Along the lines of being a trusted advisor, when you approach requests as opportunities to be of service, you are letting people know that you are a valuable resource.

First, always acknowledge the request. Repeat what your colleague asked, "You need some assistance on Saturday to move your office from the basement in your house to the new space you just leased?"

Next, deeply appreciate your colleague for asking you, "Thank you for including me. What a great opportunity for us to spend some time together. You know how much I love organizing things."

Then say, "No, that won't work for me," in a neutral and firm tone. No need to be mean spirited, just say it won't work for you.

"Oh please," she begs, "I really need your help. Why can't you help me? I would help you."

Simply repeat, "No that won't work for me."

Notice there is no excuse or story or anything after saying, "No, that won't work for me."

The moment you give a reason for saying no, your colleague can start negotiating with you, helping you overcome your objections, and convincing you to help her move her office.

Once she understands that you are not available to fulfill that request, propose a counteroffer or refer her to someone who can assist. "You know, I have a friend who owns a truck and has a stronger back that I do; he would probably be willing to help. Do you want me to ask for you?"

If your friend only wants your help and

is unwilling to accept any substitutions, then negotiate an alternative. "You know I really can't help you on Saturday, but I am available Friday for a few hours. And I can come on Sunday to help you organize."

Managing Your Team

You may have left a full-time job to start your business and if you are anything like me, you probably left because you were tired of working for other people. I often felt like I could do a better job than my manager was doing. As long as I wanted to be employed, however, I kept my attitude in check and did what was asked of me.

As your business grows and you are spending more time with clients and less time on everything else, you may find that your systems are not working as well as they used to. Additionally, it may be time to hire someone to do tasks such as managing your social media or bookkeeping. Once you start paying other people to do things that you used to do for yourself, you have a team.

Your team may consist of a virtual assistant and various other contractors who help you promote and deliver all your wonderfulness; it could also be a committee or team you are leading related to a client project, or a board you join. No matter who they are, if you are in a leadership role, you will need to make requests and oversee the people fulfilling those requests. Understanding your Personality Type could help you tap into your strengths and understand your assumptions about leadership and followship.

The people we manage, supervise, or lead, often default to a strange compromise between whatever power dynamic they grew up with and their natural style. Younger professionals tend to rely on the dynamics of their origin family. If they have an authoritarian parent, for example, they may tend to relinquish their personal power; if they had a conciliatory parent, they may not act with the level of urgency you expected; if their parents were their "friends," they may expect to discuss everything and negotiate the smallest details.

No matter the expectations and power dynamic, however, just because someone agrees to a task, does not mean they will do it when and how you expected. Most people will say yes to your requests because it's their "job" to do so. Just because they say yes, does not mean they want to say yes.

Your role in these relationships is to learn how to make clear requests and get the agreement you need. Their role is to get the clarity they need and to be honest about their ability to deliver.

When you are in a leadership role, be sure to communicate your expectations about timelines, end results, and processes. Encourage questions. The clearer they are about the request, the more likely they are to deliver the results you want. If you have not sorted all the bits, use the exchange to get clarity. At the start, this will feel contrived and difficult, but remember everything you do for the first time feels contrived. With practice you will get better and it will feel more natural.

This process is not easy. If you have limited management experience, this may test you in unexpected ways. Learning about leadership via books, seminars, and your natural leadership style can help, but theory can only take you so far. Accept that you will make mistakes and do your best to keep your sense of humor as you develop your leadership and management skills.

Throughout the first ten years that I was in business, I had a business partner. Our idea of success at the time was to expand our services and add staff. At our apex, we had a staff of seven, including ourselves. I assumed the operations management role, which included creating and implementing systems, overseeing the bookkeeper, and managing the staff. I vacillated between being overwhelmed and overbearing to cajoling people into using my systems. My management skills improved over time, but I didn't like being a manager. I wanted to provide services to my clients not track down paperwork and payroll details.

When my partner and I ended our business relationship, I rearranged the business so that I only needed a part-time assistant. I soon discovered that I was a better manager and a happier business owner. You see, at the time I felt obliged to keep adding employees because I believed that's what it meant to be successful. That obligation was at the root of my feeling overwhelmed; it kept me from being the respectful and inclusive manager I wanted to be.

In retrospect, I understand that managing the administrative operations of the business was a terrible use of me; my behaviors were classic signs of stress for a person with my Personality Type. I have hired and supervised multiple bookkeepers, assistants, and other contractors throughout these many years. I like collaborating with others and am energized by talking through ideas. I don't like tracking details and managing operations. I am not always as clear as I need to be, I am often frustrated that other people have not read my mind, and I am mostly able to keep my sense of humor about it all.

Handling Difficult Conversations

Learning to handle confrontation will help you be a stronger negotiator in all areas of your life. Whether you are the confronter or the confronted, your ability to managing the situation will help you build confidence and stamina as you grow your business

If you need to confront another person about their behavior or performance, you can dramatically lower the tension by how you set the stage. Start by acknowledging that the situation is stressful; this will immediately help everyone start breathing again. Keep your language as direct, factual, and calm as possible. Focus on the issue at hand; no need to bring up past issues and tangential situations. Treat the other person like a human being; listen to their concerns and address them early in the conversation. Balance what you say but be sure the message is loud and clear. And be sure to refer to your future working relationship to help them understand what to expect next.

Before initiating a difficult conversation, reduce your own stress as much as possible. Purge feelings beforehand if possible. You can always vent to a neutral party. This can help you get to the root of your frustration or better articulate the issue at hand. Do your homework: get your facts together and keep them handy during the conversation. Think through what you want from the conversation. What is your bottom line? What do you expect or want from the other person? Consider the other person's perspective, objections, and reactions. Anticipate your responses. Build in back up; have someone who can both commiserate and strategize.

If you are the person being confronted, you can reduce the stress by how you respond. Remember the person confronting you is likely nervous and uncomfortable, too. Do your best to listen all the way to the end of the concern before saying a word. Maintain as much eye contact as you can manage. Ask clarifying questions and ask for examples. If no remedy or course of action is mentioned, ask for input. Be willing to admit your part in the problem, apologize, and negotiate if it's warranted.

Before walking into a difficult conversation, take care of yourself. Play the "what if" game with someone else; consider the worst that can happen. Talk about your fears and identify the source of your fears. Imagine different scenarios and remind yourself that you will survive and rise another day. Understand your boundaries and limits, articulate what is acceptable to you. Breathe in and out.

If either party in a negotiation feels agitated, annoyed, or pushed around, it will show up in body language, tone of voice, and facial expressions. The shift may be subtle or dramatic, but it's a sign that at least one party is angry. Taking a break is the fastest and easiest way to shift the energy. The break could last minutes or days. The most important part is breaking the tension in the moment.

When you reconvene, seek common ground and make it overt. Discuss what you agree upon openly. The smallest bit of agreement can give you toe hold and lead to more agreement. Remember, everyone is at least 10% right.

The Most Difficult Conversation

One of the most difficult conversations I ever had was negotiating the separation from my business partner. You see, he was not just my business partner; he was and still is my husband. We had been arguing and throwing around various threats of separating for a couple of years and it bled into our social life, our vacations, and the foundation of our marriage.

Each time he threatened to leave the business and take his clients and revenues with him, I conceded and promised to run the business differently. Eventually I would grow frustrated and revert to the way I liked to do things. When we finally faced the reality that we could no longer be business partners, we were both terrified and exhausted. Neither one of us knew if our marriage could withstand a dissolution of our business partnership. We had been in business longer than we had been married and we lost track of where one started and the other began.

Facing the truth allowed us to find common ground, forgive indiscretions, and de-escalate the anger. In the end, we created a remarkably simple separation agreement and went on our different business ways. I kept the original corporate name and structure, and he formed a new company with two other consultants. The first couple of years were the hardest. We didn't talk about the details of our businesses for a long time; we needed time for the wounds to heal and to discover our marriage again.

In many ways, it was like starting a new business for each of us. We each had the opportunity to create the business we wanted and to manage it independently. It was exhilarating and scary and exciting, and sometimes very lonely. Looking back from where I am now, however, I wouldn't change a thing.

Not only surviving but thriving after that difficult conversation, I am not intimidated by confronting difficulties. I know that no matter how uncomfortable or even scary they feel in the moment, there is a way through. It takes time, compassion, and humor.

10
How Do I Set Myself Up for Success?

Remember when we started this process and we looked at your skills, talents, and qualifications? Well, it's time to revisit those with a wiser eye. I asked you to lump your skills, talents, and qualifications into three basic categories: marketing, finance, and operations and notice where your natural strengths are.

If you didn't sort your skills, talents, and qualifications into these three buckets, take a moment to do that now. Next, rank your strengths. Of these three areas, where are your Superpowers? Where are your Bozopowers?

Lean into your strengths, even if that area is a mix of skills, talents, and qualifications. As I said before, marketing is my strongest area, operations rank second, and finance is third. I tend to spend most of my non-billable time in marketing. I am energized by meeting with people, building my referral network, and generally promoting my business. I can get periodically obsessive with establishing operational systems and I use them to keep myself organized so that I can spend more time on marketing.

My favorite activity, however, is helping clients create the lives they love. It's the highest and best use of my talents and qualification; the more time and energy I devote to that, the more fulfilled I am. I didn't become an entrepreneur to manage an office, supervise staff, and maintain finances. Helping people have better lives and businesses is what motivates me, and that guiding light helps me know when to hire help.

Once I understood the basics of finance and realized how taxing it was for me to tend to the finances, I hired a bookkeeper. I could have overcome myself and maintained my own books, but that is a terrible use of my time; I don't know enough about taxes and accounting to handle them well. The potential for getting into trouble with the tax department, coupled with the consequences of poorly kept finances was too much of a risk. I have contracted with a bookkeeper for 25 years and don't have any plans to stop.

Hiring help didn't automatically solve all my problems. I still needed to be able to answer my bookkeepers' questions, organize my details so they could be entered properly, understand the QuickBooks reports, and know enough to recognize anomalies in the numbers. Those were painful lessons, and some continue to be challenges for me.

I have also hired administrative assistants. I like setting up systems and organizing things, but I don't like maintaining filing and data entry systems. I like creating strategies and plans for marketing campaigns, but I don't like setting up and managing those campaigns. Similar to bookkeeping, it's not a good use of my time to while away my days managing admin.

Don't even get me started on computer technology! I have about a 30-minute tolerance for keeping my sense of humor when my computer systems are not running smoothly. I have more patience with bookkeeping than I do when I have to deal with a technology issue. I knew immediately that I needed help in this area, but finding someone who I could work with effectively was a challenge. People skills are not usually well developed in tech-people; my lack of patience and humor coupled with their lack of humor about people who don't understand technology exacerbated my anxiety and rarely resolved my issues. I met my current IT fellow as part of the referral group, BNI. We were friends and colleagues before I hired him, so I knew he had good people skills and I trusted him. When he laughs in the middle of a tech support call, I know he is laughing with me, not at me. He has been helping me keep my tech sanity since 2005.

Although marketing is my strongest area, I also hire marketing help. I have good instincts about who my clients are and what messages will effectively engage their attention, but I have hired various marketing professionals to help me get in front my potential clients more effectively. I conceptualized and wrote all the copy for my website, but I hired a web designer to bring it into being. You see, while marketing is my strength, I am not a marketing expert and I need help.

Use your strengths as the entry point into launching and growing your business. Add and learn new skills as you need them. Because I am generally an obsessively curious person, I am constantly learning new skills. I have spent hundreds of hours taking workshops, watching tutorials, and reading books, articles, and how-to-wikis. But I am not a random learner. I dove deeply into the technical aspects of video recording because it served a higher need: communicating with my audience and enhancing my ability to serve clients. I've spent too many hours researching office chairs and ergonomic keyboards so that I could spend less time on recovering from cramped shoulders and a tired back and more time on serving clients. I even figured out how to organize my accounting details for my bookkeeper so that she interrupts me less often while I am serving clients.

You get the idea, right? When I notice that I am spending too much time and energy on something that interferes with my ability to help people have better lives and businesses, I take the time and energy to remedy it.

Since I have managed to stay in business all these years, I have a lot more forgiveness for my blind spots and have more humor about asking for assistance. I used to give myself a really hard time about being a Bozo with financials, for example. It was a source of shame and has cost me a lot of money over the years. Developing a sense of humor about being a human being has soothed the imagined egoic wounds.

I am fortunate that my husband's reliable skills are in the financial arena. I lean into his strengths on a regular basis, and he has helped me untangle several financial snarls that my lack of knowledge would have made worse. His blind spot is marketing, by the way, so he has leaned heavily on my talents since the time we were business partners.

Lean into your Superpowers. Learn new skills as you need them. And hire help to compensate for your Bozopowers!

Trust Your Superpowers!

Lead the process with your Superpowers and build in support for your Bozopowers. The more you honor your strengths or talents as you create and build your business, the more likely you are to stay in business. Remember my first forays into business? I was using too many skills and not enough talents. There is nothing inherently wrong about making clothing for others, but it was not sustainable or fulfilling for me.

While there are many nuances to understanding your Personality Type, I have discovered there are four basic entrepreneurial styles.

- **Efficient Structure Types:**
  - ✓ Tend to bring a corporate energy to their projects and are typically drawn toward environments in which they can create, implement, and manage systems and standards.
  - ✓ Thrive in roles where their practical and aspirational logical system expertise is in demand.
  - ✓ Find comfort in predictability, documented procedures, and cost-effective operations.

- **Precise Systems Types:**
  - ✓ Tend to bring an exploratory energy to their projects and are typically drawn toward environments in which they can solve complex challenges.
  - ✓ Thrive in roles in which they get to apply unconventional approaches to solving immediate and systemic problem.
  - ✓ Find comfort in ever-shifting variables that present problems to be solved, including negotiating deals.

- **Empathetic Harmony Types:**
  - ✓ Tend to bring a caretaking energy to their projects and are typically drawn to toward environments in which they can improve the physical, emotional, and spiritual needs of the people involved.
  - ✓ Thrive in roles in which they are attuned with people and can provide practical and aspirational advice regarding human relations.
  - ✓ Find comfort in knowing that the people they serve are striving toward harmonious lives, individually and within groups.

- **Personal Authenticity Types:**
  - ✓ Tend to bring a passionate energy to their projects and are typically drawn toward environments in which they can alleviate the suffering for an underserved population.
  - ✓ Thrive in roles in which they are fully aligned so their creative capacity is completely open to address immediate and systemic issues.
  - ✓ Find comfort in seeking a deep alignment between the core values that fuel their passions and their clients.

These brief descriptions are a starting point. If you want to understand the depth and breadth of your Personality Type, please contact me directly.

Legal Structures & Finances are Intimate Partners

Speaking of Bozopowers, unless your professional services are centered on accounting or legal advising, diving into the deep end with financial and legal matters is probably not what is compelling you to launch a business. The legal aspects of establishing your business are often the most intimidating to new business owners; accounting is a close second.

These are two of my least favorite and two of the most important aspects of starting and growing a business. Since accounting and legal are intricately tied to each other, it may help to consider them as dance partners. There you go, learning about a new dance!

While starting a business is likely a deeply personal decision, it is also a significant financial and legal decision. Which kind of legal structure you select has a direct impact on both your business and personal finances. For example, the option of being a sole proprietor may seem like the obvious choice due to the minimal legal paperwork involved. In most states within the US, for example, you just need to register the name of your business and declare yourself a sole proprietor and *voilà*, you've "launched."

For consultants who make more than $50,000 in yearly gross revenues, however, this selection can result in payment of ridiculously high levels of self-employment taxes. Most consultants operate as Limited Liability Companies (LLCs) because this structure offers a higher degree of flexibility. If you want to clearly declare your commitment to Corporate Social Responsibility, you may consider registering as a Benefit Corporation, or B Corp.

Remember I joined a company that was already established, and it was a Sub S-Corporation (S-Corp). The LLC option was not yet available in Vermont and the S-Corp structure worked for the two people who started the business. When I became the sole owner of the corporation, I considered changing the status to an LLC. At first blush, it seemed like an easier structure to manage, but upon further research, I decided to remain an S-Corp.

When the B Corps option became available in Vermont, I looked into this, too. I am attracted to the concept and values reflected in declaring my company a B-Corp. However, when I did the research, I discovered there are some complexities to becoming and maintaining B-Corp status and I didn't find the values to be a compelling enough reason to change.

The S-Corp structure allows the owners of the company to be employees, which means they don't pay self-employment taxes on their gross revenues. My company gives me a paycheck, pays rent to me (the property owner of the building), and at the end of the year the overall profit or loss of the company is folded into my personal income. Some years I pay taxes on the profit; other years I get a refund because of the loss.

My previous entrepreneurial endeavors were Sole Proprietorships because I was intimidated by what seemed like complicated legal paperwork and didn't know enough to ask for help.

If you're having some trouble tracking all of this, not to worry. With a little research all of this will make more sense. The most important criteria for selecting your legal structure is understanding the financial impacts on your household.

It's worth the time and money to talk to a lawyer familiar with Solopreneurial start-ups before registering your business with the Secretary of State. If you have already declared your legal structure and want to change it, the good news is that you don't have to get it perfect the first time; you can change your legal structure as your business grows.

Many attorneys who specialize in business have "start-up packages" to help you steer and document your business for a reasonable fee. Depending on the state or country where you will be doing business, you may not require a lawyer to file all the paperwork, but an hour or two of legal advice can help you navigate the process more effectively. Before meeting with a legal advisor and starting the $250+ per hour clock running, take the time to educate yourself with the basics so you get the most from that premium priced advice.

Start by opening the official website of the state or country where your business will be "domiciled," or headquartered. Find the Secretary of State (or the equivalent of this in your country) and read. Read as much as you can. Take notes and prepare some questions. Other resources in the US include the Small Business Administration (SBA), especially the women's business center office of the SBA.

Every state in the US is mandated to have a business center specifically for women. Look for local business organizations and trade groups that provide what is called "technical assistance" for small businesses and sign up for webinars, classes, or meet with an advisor. Mostly ask a lot of what may seem like obvious questions and get comfortable with the lingo. The more informed and comfortable you are, the more effective your meeting with an attorney will be.

Simultaneously, find a good tax accountant who specializes in start-ups and pay for an hour of two of their expertise. Bring the last few years of federal and state taxes and other financial paperwork for them to review at the meeting. And ask a lot of questions. You need to understand the financial consequences of choosing one legal structure over another. Even if you insist on processing your own taxes and never talk to that person again, this is an important investment and a crucial step in understanding your options. While a tax accountant cannot and should not ethically tell you what kind of legal structure to select, they can help you make an informed decision.

Self Employed, Business Owner, Entrepreneur?

It's common to use many different terms interchangeably when referring to privately owned businesses. Some of these terms are strictly defined by the tax department and others are not. Knowing these terms will help you select a term that best fits how you see your business. The following is intended to help you find the language that suits you.

- **Small Business:** A business with up to 500 employees technically defines a small business. Most small businesses have 100 or fewer employees and are in all sectors of the economy.
- **Micro-enterprise:** A business operating on a small scale, usually with a sole owner and fewer than six employees.
- **Entrepreneur:** A person who organizes, manages, and assumes the risks of a business or enterprise. Usually started with the intent of adding employees, expanding products and services, and potentially adding locations.
- **Solopreneur:** A person who sets up and operates a business on their own. Usually started with the intent of maintaining all operational functions by one person with some contracted assistance (administrative, technical, bookkeeping, etc.).
- **Lifestyle Business:** A business established by its founders primarily with the aim of sustaining a particular level of income and no more, or to provide a foundation from which to enjoy a particular lifestyle. Tend to depend heavily on the founder's skills, personality, energy, and contacts. Usually associated with services rather than products.
- **Freelancer:** A person who accepts projects related to their skills and talents without a long-term commitment to any one employer. Usually associated with people offering creative services.
- **Independent Contractor:** A person who provides services to another person or company under agreed upon terms (time, location, price, etc.). This also implies that the person or company paying for the services is not paying any taxes associated with the service providers payroll taxes.

A Brief Dance Lesson on Legal Structures

Each type of legal structure offers a different level of legal protection and has different impacts on your personal finances; just like dancing with a partner, it takes two to Tango.

The following is NOT intended as legal advice, but rather to give you an idea of each type of corporation so you can start asking more questions.

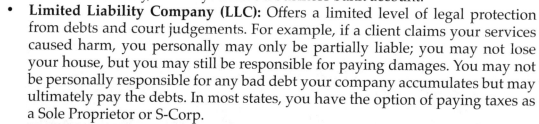

- **Sole Proprietor:** Simplest form of business, offers no protection for personal assets against any potential legal action. For example, if a client claims your services caused harm, you personally will be held legally liable for any financial or criminal damages. Personal and business income are taxed as one entity, even if you have a business bank account.

- **Limited Liability Company (LLC):** Offers a limited level of legal protection from debts and court judgements. For example, if a client claims your services caused harm, you personally may only be partially liable; you may not lose your house, but you may still be responsible for paying damages. You may not be personally responsible for any bad debt your company accumulates but may ultimately pay the debts. In most states, you have the option of paying taxes as a Sole Proprietor or S-Corp.

- **Limited Liability Partnership (LLP):** Similar to an LLC but requires at least one partner.

- **Sub S- Corporation (S-Corp):** Offers more legal protection; you and any additional owners are "shareholders" of the company. You won't lose your house, but you are financially responsible for any debts your business incurs. When it comes time to file taxes, only the shareholders' personal taxes are affected; the company pays no taxes on profits. This means any profit or loss generated by the business "passes through" your personal taxes and depending on other aspects of your personal finances, can either result in you personally paying taxes on the profit or receiving a tax refund.

- **C-Corporation (C-Corp):** Offers the highest level of legal protection. Since corporations (in the US) are considered "individual taxpayers," a disgruntled client can sue the company and you are not personally liable. The company assets are up for grabs, but your personal assets are protected. Since a corporation is an entity, it pays taxes on its own profit; you pay taxes on any income or financial compensation you may have received from the company as an employee or shareholder.

- **Benefit Corporation (B-Corp):** Similar to C-Corps regarding the legal and financial exposure but provides a different structure for shareholder decision-making power. Legally, when a C-Corp is sold, the sale has to provide the highest possible financial advantage to the shareholders. Owners of a B Corp, however, can negotiate a sale based on factors beyond financial gain, such as the benefit to the community and/or the environment. B-corps also have specific measurements of corporate social responsibility built into their governance.

The above information is NOT intended as legal advice, but rather to give you an idea of each type of corporation so you can start asking more questions.

Am I a Contractor or a Consultant?

This may not seem like an important distinction, but please take a moment to understand the differences between contracting and consulting; it will impact how you frame your services and ultimately how you price them.

If you are leading a project that requires you to be on-site for three days a week, for example, and you suddenly find yourself showing up every day for weeks on end, you are likely becoming a contractor and leaving the role of consultant. And it's time to renegotiate your agreement or contract with that client.

Since for many years the federal government made no distinction between contractors and consultants, it is easy to cross the line without realizing it. Crossing that line can have significant tax consequences for you and your client. Contractors are a legally separate class now. If you start to look and smell a lot like an employee, you are a contractor not a consultant and can be taxed differently on your income.

- Contractors tend to become a part of the organization and stick around longer.
- Consultants advise, teach, coach, mentor, and exit.
- Most organizations are not willing to pay a consulting daily rate for more than a few weeks because it gets expensive fast. If a client wants to negotiate your daily or hourly rate, proceed with caution; you may be at risk of becoming a pseudo employee without the benefits of being a full-time employee. The Federal and State governments have various guidelines to distinguish between contractors and employees. Many states have different interpretations of the Federal rules. It's important that you understand the differences and know the law in your state.
- In casual conversation, many people use terms like *contractor* and *consultant* interchangeably and include a wide array of people who are not employees. Keep these distinctions described below in mind as you navigate.
- If you are performing tasks that other employees perform or are integral to the products or services that the organization provides to their customers, such as sourcing raw materials for a computer component manufacturer, you are an employee and should be included in their payroll and benefits program.
- If you are providing a service that no one else in the organization performs, such as IT management for that computer component manufacturer over many months or years, you are likely a contractor.
- If you are advising that same manufacturer on how to set up, manage, and train their staff in maintaining their data management system, you are likely a consultant.

Pay attention to the details, monitor projects, and discuss changes as soon as you notice them. Most clients are not intentionally trying to slip one past you; most people don't really know the differences and it's easy for a project to start as one thing and transition into another.

Tending Your Books

On the surface, software packages like QuickBooks, FreshBooks, or any other comprehensive product can make bookkeeping and accounting seem simple; you track what you earn and spend and *tada*! . . .you know if you made a profit or not.

It's that easy and it's not.

Even if you cannot afford to hire a bookkeeper to enter all your transactions, I highly recommend that you hire an accountant to help you set up your bookkeeping system; it will save you thousands of dollars in the future when you have to hire someone to unsnarl the rat's nest you may have created because you didn't fully understand the complexities of accounting.

Don't be lulled into complacency by simply "following the directions" and "answering all the introductory questions." There are nuances and subtleties that a trained professional can guide you through that will make a big difference and will save you money, time, and lots of frustration.

When I computerized my manual bookkeeping system many moons ago, I purchased QuickBooks and was lulled into bliss by answering all the introductory questions. It looked so easy. The software translated my questions into something called a *chart of accounts*. I only had a general idea of what a chart of accounts was anyway, so it looked good to me. I proceeded to enter receipts, generate invoices, record deposits, and print tidy little reports that gave me the confidence that all was good and well. Since my husband, who was my business partner at the time, also did our taxes, using a software package that asked lots of easy-to-answer questions, we believed that we were doing great as long as the numbers looked good on paper.

As I became busier with clients and had less time for administrative tasks, the bookkeeping piles started taking over my desk and sliding onto the floor. I felt obligated to enter all the data arduously and dutifully. It felt like a defeat to admit that I couldn't do it.

The truth was, I could do it *and* I didn't want to. I used to carry it back and forth from the office and home, thinking I would get to it at night. I even tried getting up early to tackle it. When I finally admitted that I wasn't going to do it and needed to hire someone, it was too close to tax time to have someone else do it. That year we decided to hand tally our numbers and cram them through the tax software to file our taxes on time.

I had reached my limit on both my desire to maintain the system and my capacity to focus on accounting as our business was growing. It was ultimately a really bad use of my time; I was slow and made mistakes and needed to focus on higher-level tasks.

After our first bookkeeper reduced the piles and put order into my life again, she asked me questions such as why I categorized certain items as business expenses when they were really shareholder distributions. I didn't know what a shareholder distribution was.

Bottom line was, I had been making many small and medium-sized mistakes for years and was lucky that I never got audited by the tax department. The Internal Revenue Service doesn't care that you are not a professional bookkeeper or that you just answered the questions in QuickBooks.

The Basics Are Not So Basic

At the most fundamental level, business bookkeeping is a lot like managing your personal bank account. You need to know how much money you have coming in and you need to know what your expenses are. As long as your expenses don't exceed your income, you will generally be ok.

But business expenses are really different from personal expenses and this is why having an accountant help you set up your system makes a difference. While software systems come with some fundamentals installed, they are based on assumptions of what the average professional service business needs. Since you are an individual and will vary from the average in many aspects, those assumptions may complicate your life.

If you don't know the difference between an operating cost and a start-up cost, you may miss some important tax advantages. Start-up costs include what you initially purchase to launch and the value of all the items you brought into the business. You may already have a home office, for example, so you just start using it for your new business. Well, all of the furnishings, office supplies, computer equipment, and books you already had on the first day of business, could be considered business assets and their value can be claimed as start-up costs. Anything new you purchase or acquire to start could go into that bucket too. Your start-up costs are assets, also known as your personal investment in your business, and if you decide to close your business, the company may owe you personally the equivalent monetary value of that asset.

Operating costs are all your expenses after you launch. Even if you buy a new computer a year after launching, it is considered an operating cost, because it cost you money to buy that computer so you can operate your business. Some operating costs are depreciable expenses, and some are fixed. Office furnishings and equipment generally depreciate in value, as their monetary value decreased from year to year and are counted as losses; paper clips and printer paper are fixed.

Not all fixed expenses are equal, either. You can only claim 30% off lunch at the corner market because the tax department figures you have to eat anyway. Just because you happened to be working, they allow for a few crumbs. Paying for lunch with a potential client, however, could be 100% expensed if you claim it as a marketing expense. Yes, you happened to eat lunch while marketing your business, but it can also be a marketing tactic, aka networking.

Many professional service businesses start in an extra room of the house or a corner of the living room. Even if you are not technically renting office space, there are tax benefits to claiming your extra room as an in-home office. Each state has its own variations on the details, but the IRS allows you to take a percentage of your home mortgage, energy bills, and other costs of owning a home as a business expense. If you rent an office and have a home office, however, you can't claim both. If you own a commercial building and rent from yourself, your rent check is a business expense and the rental income you deposit into your personal checking account is not payroll taxable but is part of your gross personal income.

When relocating the business in 1998, my husband and I intentionally purchased a residential home with an attached office suite that has a separate external entrance for clients and deliveries. We divided the 700 square feet into a private office for each of us, a reception area where in-person clients could wait, and an office supply and copier room. It allows us to essentially work from home with the feeling of being away from home and presents a more professional image to clients. Since we own the property, our business rents office space from us, the property owners, providing us with an additional income stream from the business.

Paying yourself may seem straightforward, but that can get complicated fast if you aren't careful. It all depends on the legal structure you selected. As a sole proprietor, you could take a "draw" and pay quarterly estimated taxes, which may be easy to calculate if you pay yourself the same amount every week or month. As an S-Corp, you are both a shareholder and an employee of the company and can receive paychecks and other forms of cash compensation. Paychecks get social security, unemployment taxes, and other items subtracted from the gross amount, depending on where you live; year-end profit sharing does not. And when your company issues a paycheck to you personally, the company pays half of those deductions and the other half comes out of your paycheck. So, if you are the sole employee, you are essentially paying both halves of the payroll taxes. Then there is the filing!

I know you are thinking that there must be software that can do all this. Yes, there is. And you need to set it up properly or those tidy little reports you submit will not match what the IRS has calculated, and you'll find yourself in a painful battle of resubmitting forms and responding to multiple form letters from the IRS.

And by the way, all of this is easier when you maintain a separate bank account for your business. Even if you are a sole-proprietor and it seems unnecessarily complicated, keep a dedicated business account. Not only will it help you run a cleaner operation, but it will also help you know the actual financial details of your business and on the off chance that you are audited, need to apply for credit or a grant, or want to sell your business you will be grateful for the separation of accounts.

I know many Solopreneurs who were not able to access the generous grants doled out by the Federal government during the COVID era. They were generally Bozo in the accounting area, had not hired help, and had not kept their accounting records updated. If COVID had struck just a few years earlier, I would have been in the same boat. We had been without bookkeeping assistance for a year and our accounting was a mess.

Have Some Business Insurance for Good Measure

While you're at it, talk to your insurance agent about the basic coverage you need as a consultant. I am not a fan of having insurance for the sake of insurance, but a little bit can go a long way for most professional service providers. It may be as easy as adding a clause to your homeowners or apartment rental insurance policy.

Remember that an insurance agent's job is to sell insurance, so just as you did your research before meeting with an attorney or accountant, gather your information. At a minimum, ask other professional service providers what kind of insurance they have and why. Their *why* is as important as their *what* when it comes to insurance.

Some government agencies, for example, require that all vendors maintain some form of liability insurance. When I needed to show proof of insurance to the state of Vermont, I simply sent their insurance criteria to my agent and asked to be covered for those specific items, nothing more. Because I continue to do business with the state, I maintain that coverage.

As with most legal and financial aspects of your business, ask a lot of questions, gather useful information, and make the best-informed decision you can make.

Hire Good People

I have hired more than a dozen different bookkeepers. Some had a bit of accounting experience and helped clean up messes, others were really basic bookkeepers who simply entered the data, still others were glorified office assistants and caused some problems; some were very expensive, and others were suspiciously cheap. I have kept some bookkeepers for years on end, while asking others not to return after their first day.

What I know now is that hiring the right person makes all the difference. Finding someone who cares as much about getting the numbers right as you do is key. Just because someone is highly recommended does not mean they are a good bookkeeper for you. If you don't like working with that person or have any random concerns, find a different person. Your bookkeeper will be up close and personal to the tiniest details of your life; make sure you trust them and feel completely comfortable with that level of intimacy.

After a succession of bookkeepers who did not stick, I hired a person who recently left a corporate accounting position and was launching her own business. I was attracted to her higher-level skills and imagined that she would be able to finally clean up several lingering messes in my system. In the end, she was a terrible fit and caused huge issues.

She is an accountant, not a bookkeeper. While she is smart and competent at what she does, she did not know some important details. She had only ever supervised other people who processed payroll; she didn't know the intricacies of filing reports with the State and Federal tax departments. And again, she had supervised accounts payable and accounts receivable clerks but had never done the entry herself. Two years after she left to take a full-time position with another company, we were still cleaning up messes and disputing fines with the IRS.

Unfortunately, her departure coincided with a busy time for me, and I didn't have the bandwidth to find a replacement. Weeks became months and the piles mounted. I considered doing the entry myself but never did. I asked my part-time assistant to do some entry, but she didn't know enough to be effective without a lot of supervision.

I occasionally organized the piles to keep them from littering my office floor. Six months into shuffling the piles, I initated a search for a bookkeeper and discovered there was a shortage of qualified people in my area.

As the search stretched into months, the piles became mountains. When I finally hired a new bookkeeper, she enthusiastically and diligently made mole hills of those mountains. Between September and December, she came to my office twice a month to enter thousands of bits of data for three different companies with multiple bank accounts.

I worked closely with her to answer questions and explain my quirky systems. I quickly saw that she asked good questions, knew how to research issues I couldn't resolve, and mostly she kept her sense of humor as I moved through varying levels of angst and panic. She is more expensive than any other bookkeeper I've hired, but she is worth every cent because she is competent, admits when she doesn't know the answer, is glad to research mysteries, and cares as much about my business as I do.

Being without bookkeeping support for most of 2018, reminded me how vitally important this role is. Even though I didn't enter any of the data, the whole process took a lot of my energy and time. Given that this is my least favorite activity, I have been much happier since hiring my current bookkeeping angel.

Hiring competent help can save you thousands of dollars. I have paid thousands of dollars in fines, penalties, and late fess to the IRS and the State of Vermont because I did not have a professional to help me set up the financial tasks correctly. Remember my accountant who didn't understand payroll? Well, here is the rest of the story.

After hours on the phone, months of letters back and forth, new forms filed, and more checks written, the IRS was still not convinced we were even. Letter upon letter that detailed growing fines and interest on the original fines filled the mailbox. Months later, all the paperwork finally caught up with itself and an actual human being reviewed and reconciled all the bits. In the end, the IRS issued two final letters. These letters were attached to a check for $9000 and another for $3000 from the IRS for overpayment. I had a good laugh and immediately deposited them.

I trust that you can see how important it is to have reliable professional help to sort through these variables. The money you spend to get good professional advice to launch, by the way, is a start-up cost; your bookkeeper is an operating expense.

Please don't assume any of these ideas presented here are immediately applicable to your business. Don't fall into the trap of thinking that since you are really smart you can figure it all out on your own. I know you are really smart; I am, too. My Superpowers are best used in serving clients, marketing and growing my business, and hiring good help; accounting and taxes are my kryptonite.

I know people who manage all their own bookkeeping, file all their own reports, and file their own annual taxes. They have not spent hours sorting out IRS messes and they have never been audited. I bow down to them with great respect. If, however, finance is one of your Bozopowers, please do yourself a favor and hire a professional!

Do You Need an Accountant or a Bookkeeper?

Bookkeepers and accountants often do the same physical work of entering information and generating reports, but there are some key differences. Simply put, bookkeepers generally record transactions and keep you financially organized, while accountants provide consultation, analysis, and more qualified to advise on tax matters.

Accountants tend to cost more to hire and are best used for taxes and strategic planning.

A good bookkeeper can save you money because your accountant will have reliable information and spend less time organizing your details.

If you already have an accountant, ask them for a referral for bookkeepers they know. Trust me, they will be thrilled when a professional, instead of you, is finally entering all the data they have to sort through at the end of the year.

Create an Advisory Team

Beyond hiring people to compensate for your blind spots, consider forming an advisory team. An advisory team is more than a few good friends who want to see you succeed. It is more like a group of professional peers who have different talents, reliable skills, and blind spots than you. You may assemble them into a formal group and meet regularly as a team; you may also meet with each one individually as needed. Your team will likely be a mix of people you pay, the way you pay an accountant and lawyer, and people in your referral network such as non-competitive or complimentary professional service providers.

My advisory team has evolved from being formal to less formal throughout the years, but I know who to call when I need assistance with an aspect of my business that is troubling me. Having been in business for many years, I have collected quite a few professional peers as friends and we often share insights, bounce ideas off each other, and learn from each other's challenges and triumphs.

These peers have helped me revamp my approach to negotiating contracts, raise my prices without scaring away potential clients, be more effective with non-profit clients, learn new technologies, discover new tools and resources that help me serve clients better, and much more. Remember that a key aspect to establishing and maintaining a strong peer network is to ask others to be a resource and be a resource to others. People who are good at what they do love sharing their expertise with others, so ask away.

I have also hired coaches and consultants to support goals such as developing a strategic, rather than random, social media promotional plan; or writing and publishing a book; or helping me set up my office systems to be more effective for how I work. Since all of these folks were already part of my professional network, I trusted them and knew the quality of their work. But instead of asking for free advice and potentially abusing our relationship, I hired them to let them know I respect them and want to compensate them for their expertise.

Discerning when it's appropriate to just pick a professional peer's brain or when you need to hire them depends a lot on the level of your relationship and how much picking is involved. A few casual questions at a mixer are fine; cornering someone at a mixer, opening your website on your phone, and asking for their analysis is too much. Getting to know a new person over lunch or coffee and asking for their perspective on the on-line technology they use is great; asking them to come to your office to train you in that technology for free is probably asking too much. Asking a long-time colleague to help you reflect on your business strategy in exchange for a free lunch is good; asking that same person to read your 50-page strategic plan and give you annotated feedback is too much. You see, it's about balancing the size of the ask with the depth of relationship.

I hire people when I want their undivided attention and when it involves my blind spot skills, when I want a real professional job and when I want accountability to myself on the results. I often offer to pay close friends for their services to respect their time and expertise and am glad to pay their hourly rate. Some refuse payment and others graciously accept; I leave that decision to them to reconcile. And just because someone declines payment the first time that I ask for help, does not mean I don't offer the next time. Be respectful of other people's time and expertise and others will be respectful of your time and expertise.

I have always had legal counsel, financial support from a bookkeeper and a tax accountant, and some form of a coach on my paid team. I recommend you keep at least legal and financial counsel on hand.

Since we are talking about networks, remember to tend to yours. Deepen active connections and broaden into new ones whenever you are at an event or are part of a group. Listen for opportunities to meet one-to-one with people who you admire, respect, or about whom you are simply curious. Develop and maintain your referral network by keeping them informed, coaching them on how to refer more primary customers more effectively, and thanking them for their support.

Networking may feel like a part-time job when you start, but once you find your pace and style it will become a natural part of being a member of society. No one likes the smarmy insurance sales rep who gives everyone their business card, but people do like being listened to, responding to thoughtful questions, and discovering common ground. Focus on quality of connections rather than quantity and you will accumulate a wide and deep network before you know it.

Accountability Groups

A close cousin to an advisory group is an accountability group, often called a mastermind group. The Mastermind Group model, developed by Napoleon Hill in his book, *Think and Grow Rich* published in 1937, is basically a committed group of people, ideally four to six, who meet weekly or monthly, set goals, and hold each other accountable for reaching those goals.

I have been a member of numerous accountability groups, even one that involved paying monetary fines for not completing whatever I declared each week for five years. While I don't condone this kind of group now, I did learn how to make clear goals with clear deadlines and accomplish them. I also learned how to write things in such a way that the result could be broadly interpreted and over time those broad interpretations diluted the intent of monetary accountability. In the end, I did master the ability to "make s–t happen" like nobody's business. I don't need or want that kind of accountability anymore.

Meeting weekly, while advised in the Mastermind model, is not always practical for Solopreneurs. Once or twice a month allows for a bit more grace when unexpected events derail your good intentions. In person is more powerful than phone or live video and generally takes more time out of the day. Shared or rotating meeting facilitation is ideal and not always effective. Four members are good and six is a more resilient number. And permission to call someone out for not meeting their goals is essential. That "calling out" can be coaching a fellow member to create goals that are attainable by mere mortals who operate in linear earth time or finding out what is in the way of the goal or discerning if the intended goal is a "should" or an actual desire. Remember, "shoulding" yourself or others for motivation is just about the most demotivating motivation there is.

Invest In Good Equipment

Beyond tapping your Superpowers, adding to your qualifications, developing your skills, and hiring out your Bozopowers, I recommend investing in the best equipment you can afford for your business. If you have a desk, computer, and printer now, use what you have, and fold them into your start-up costs. When it's time to replace them, do your research, possibly even hire an IT consultant for an hour, and buy quality hardware, software, and accessories.

Quality does not equate to brand new. There is a lot of really good equipment and furnishings on the secondary market. Larger companies are constantly upgrading their technology, furnishings, and décor. Office equipment companies have warehouses full of used equipment that you can buy or lease. Craigslist, Facebook Marketplace, and more local community-oriented sites have multiple listings for used furniture. Before buying anything used, do your homework; ask the seller a lot of questions and get as much assurance as possible that what you are buying is in good working order.

When we moved our offices into a larger space and needed several desks, chairs, and tables, we went to the local used office furniture store and selected the best items we could find. When I saw the business across the street dragging furniture to the curb and putting a "free" sign on it, I checked it out and scored a great desk. It was one of the heaviest desks I ever owned, was really sturdy, had great drawers, and was twice the size of my old desk.

The last time we updated our offices, a friend in the construction contracting business was retiring and he sold us a beautiful desk system for my office and one for the front reception area at a very reasonable price.

My first copier was a very used machine, but it was a big improvement over having to walk down the street to the local print shop to copy materials for workshops. I have picked up free printers and inexpensive tables and boxes of new office supplies by watching our hyper-local community forum, Front Porch Forum, and being the lucky first person to respond.

When it comes to computers, however, I always buy new. And it always feels painful because the cost is more than I like to spend, and the moment it is installed it's out of date. Computer equipment, like new cars, depreciates dramatically as soon as you open the box.

The Value of Adding Printers and Copiers

You've probably already figured out that printer ink is the most expensive office supply and if you produce a lot of materials as I do, you will buy a lot of printer cartridges. If you plan on printing 50 sets of an eight-page, full-color handout, using the average ink jet printer, you will be sorry. Just waiting for the pages to print is enough to make a person who is on a tight deadline feel anxious.

Maybe you think a high-quality printer is too expensive?

Do a little research on the types of ink, printing speed, ability to print double-sided, and cost of maintenance. Compare the cost of buying or leasing equipment with the cost of using a print shop or the potential loss of income from shoddy materials.

For Solopreneurs looking to save a bundle, consider used or refurbished equipment. Larger companies tend to lease and regularly upgrade printers and copiers. Remember that these days, a quality copier is really a more sophisticated printer, and some printers have the copier function incorporated. Copier dealerships sell used copiers just like car dealerships sell used cars. They are glad to work out financing and provide service contracts if you want them.

Many moons ago, when copiers were way out of my reach, I walked down the block to our local print shop to make copies. I only made copies when absolutely necessary. Along the way, I happened to make the acquaintance of the owner of the largest copier dealership in the state. We seemed to run in the same circles for a while and became friendly. When I casually commented that we were outgrowing our tiny office, he immediately said, "Must be time to add a copier." He was a salesman, after all

I jokingly responded, "Sure, do you have any for free?"

To my great surprise, he said, "Yes." He handed me his card with a note about who to call at his office an told me his warehouse manager would set me up with a trade-in machine for free. Within two days, I had a copier in my office and have never been without one since.

I currently have a fancy copier that can convert blank pieces of 11 x 17 pieces of paper into full-color, saddle stitched booklets. These are the most impressive workshop materials I have ever been able to produce. And I have never had a client complain about an additional fee once they see the materials.

If you have considered adding a copier to your office equipment, do a little research and use your negotiation skills to find something that serves your needs and doesn't break the bank.

11
How Do I Navigate the Road Ahead?

The business is registered, your website is live, you have business cards in hand, and you've arranged a space where you can work. What's next?

A lot!

Now you get to manage your business as it grows and takes you on the adventure of a lifetime. Being in business is much more than winning proposals, serving your clients, and making sure you stay out of trouble with the IRS. It is an opportunity to grow as a person, a community member, and as a citizen of the world. Along this path, you will be called to step forward in ways you never imagined possible, challenged to your limits and beyond, and hone your inner lump of coal into a brilliantly faceted diamond.

Your Operational Road Map

Throughout this process we have been revisiting your business road map; now it's time to expand your one-page document into your Operational Road Map. An operational business plan or road map is a dynamic living document and is intended to serve as a guide and reference point as you step into the daily function of developing and growing your business.

As a review, let's reflect on some key elements and check in on a few core questions.

- Has your motivation for being in business changed since you started this journey? What has changed and why? Can you clearly state the main problem you solve or issue you address? What is your USP?
- Do you understand who your primary clients are and where to find them? How have your client and service descriptions evolved?
- Have you already identified a few key people who will be the start of your referral network? Do you have some measurable sales goals? Can you pay yourself?
- Who is on your advisory team? If you have not created an advisory team, who are some prospects? When will you approach them?
- How will you get the word out? Of the various marketing and promotion methods, which three will you use the most? Remember, lean into your strengths here, start with what works for you and build into other areas.
- Do you understand your Superpowers? What is your kryptonite?
- What is still unclear? What resources do you need to build before starting?
- Where do you see yourself, your business, your life a year from now? Two years from now? Five years from now?

Remember, you don't need to have it all figured out to launch and be successful in business. Being in business is mostly about figuring it out as you go. And you don't need to be an expert in marketing, operations, and finance. Lean into your strengths, hire out your Bozopowers, and develop your skills in service to your Superpowers.

A Few More Considerations

Where Will You Work?

Where you set up your office is an important aspect of creating a life and a business that you love. It's all about balancing convenience and costs while keeping some boundaries between your life and your business.

As you consider your options, think about the details that will help you be effective. Creating a designated "office space" is a good place to start. This space could be a table or desk in the corner of your living room or in a separate room. It could be your dining room table or in the basement. No matter where it is, claim a space that is all about business. You can still answer emails from the couch or create content in bed but having a space that is your "office" will help you take yourself and your business more seriously while maintaining a personal life.

I've always had a designated office space. In the early years, we rented space in one of the many older buildings in Burlington that had been converted into incubator spaces for small businesses. We started in a tiny three-room space and as the company grew, we expanded into a 1,000 sq.ft. office space with a reception area and several offices. As our kids became teenagers and aged out of after school programs, however, we wanted more flexibility in the afternoons so that they were not home alone.

At that time, we had a part-time assistant, a contract bookkeeper, and I met most of my clients in-person. We eventually bought a house that had a separate entrance into an attached office suite. The suite had two private offices, a reception area, and a small supply room. The installation of a door in the hallway created an important physical and mental boundary between home and office.

When we were business partners, this space provided us with a good balance of privacy and community. When we split the company and he joined another group, I was alone more than I preferred. When he decided to return to that space, we renovated it and swapped office spaces.

Throughout all of these iterations, I kept several constants. I can open the doors and window to get fresh air, I have plenty of natural light, I have enough space to work on projects and meet with clients privately, my cats roam freely through the office, and I get to eat lunch in my own kitchen. I also like having the flexibility of bringing my computer into the living room to recline in my favorite chair by the wood stove in the winter and taking a call on the back deck in the summer.

What is important to you? Do you work best at a desk, in a comfy chair, or at a large table? Do you need plants and animals around you? Are you more effective in quiet isolation or do music and people talking keep you engaged? When you look away from your computer screen, do you have something beautifulupon which to rest your eyes? Does your space encourage you to move, stand, and walk on a regular basis?

One of the best parts of having my own office was the color: I painted two walls green and the other two orange – two of my favorite colors.

Start with what you have and adjust when you can. It's good practice to take a fresh look at your space and rearrange things at least every couple or few years.

How Will You Keep Yourself Healthy?

Maintaining your physical, emotional, social, spiritual, and mental health is paramount to maintaining a life in the midst of being a Solopreneur. The more you integrate regular well-being into your daily and weekly living the more likely you are to keep yourself upright and able to do the work you love. This includes having hobbies and interests outside of your business, making time for friends and family, and having a reason to move your body every day.

I confess, physical fitness is not my favorite thing. But being able to facilitate a group through a full day of training with good energy is important to me. I know that if I don't take care of my body, my ability to stand all day is compromised. I also know that if my physical well-being is diminished, I cannot garden, tend to my chickens, and enjoy the rewards of having a homestead. So, I attend exercise classes, schedule regular sessions with my Pilates teacher. I eat well, and I get a regular massage.

What are you doing to support your physical health?

Although I spend a lot of time networking, about a decade ago, I realized that I was spending more time alone than I preferred. My husband was away on business about half of the time, and I was bored from hanging around waiting for his return. I knew a lot of people but didn't feel known by very many of them.

I looked through my various contacts and made a list of women I had known for many years but with whom I had lost touch and women I only knew professionally but wanted to know better. I didn't tell any of them that I was intentionally creating a circle of women friends, I just started inviting them to lunch or having them over for a glass of wine, or buying an extra ticket for a show and inviting someone along.

All of them were glad to hear from me and reciprocated with social invitations. They range in age from early 30s to late 80s. Some are partnered, others single, and many are business owners. I gather with some in groups and others individually. I cry, laugh, shop, eat, and sometimes even travel with them. These are the people who help me stay sane.

Who is in your social circle and how can you engage with them in meaningful ways?

I have moved in and out of various spiritual practices and groups, but what has remained constant is my connection to plants and the seasonal cycles of the planet. Not raised within an organized religion, I have explored many different spiritual practices and communities, including living in an intentional spiritual community. From all of these experiences, I have created various daily, monthly, and seasonal rituals, practices, and activities that help me connect to something larger than my petty concerns. These activities remind me that I am not alone, and that my intentions and actions make a difference.

If you are not spiritually inclined, consider what keeps you connected to other people in a meaningful way. Are you curious about what makes people tick? Do you believe that your mood, thoughts, and actions impact others? Do you wonder what came before you were born and what will come after you are gone? Exploring these questions and finding your answers can help you through difficult times.

What kinds of activities help you stay connected to a bigger purpose than your own business concerns?

Bringing It All Together

Some of the answers to these questions will be immediately obvious and others may remain eternally elusive to you. Do your best to answer them based on what you know right now.

As you gather your answers, document them on an Operational Road Map. Reference this document as you create and update that fabulous website, design your logo, and as you build your network. Use this as a guide and adjust it as you discover new answers.

Take yourself on a business retreat once or twice a year and spend a day with your Operational Road Map, your year-to-date financial statements, and maybe even one or two members of your advisory team. Take a critical look at your business, lean into the expertise of your team, and make adjustments.

A business is a living being with a heart, soul, and brain. It needs regular care and feeding including an occasional spa day. No matter how busy you get, make time for an annual retreat so that you and your business can grow and prosper together.

Ready, Set, Go!

Whew! We have covered a lot of territory.

If you have followed along, considered the concepts, answered the questions, and kept your sense of humor, you are in a good place to launch, grow, and prosper as a Solopreneur. Remember, lean into your strengths, learn, and stretch into unexplored corners of your abilities, develop your network, ask for help when you need it, and hire help to compensate for your Bozopowers.

Mostly, keep your sense of humor and find companions who can help you find your sense of humor when you do lose it. Being in business for yourself will be one of the most challenging and exhilarating journeys of self-discovery you will experience. There will be many days when you will question the wisdom of launching your business. But not having a sense of humor about being a human being in the middle of designing, building, and repairing the bus as it zips down the highway will make it all a dreadfully long and arduous journey.

I can't wait to learn more about your journey. Please stay connected, include me in your network, and go forth and be your fabulous self.

Epilogue

Thank you for being brave in the face of uncertainty and allowing yourself to reflect and regroup as you moved through this journey. Thank you for joining the many millions of women who are forging their own path, defining success on their terms, and making a difference in the world.

May your journey be filled with remarkable celebrations, opportunities to gain experience, insights, and inspirations about how to serve your clients, and mostly may it be Fabulous!

While this book is chock full of powerful information and stories, there is more to growing and prospering than could ever be covered in one book. Please reach out, connect, and ask for support as you move into your next phase.

For coaching, workshops, and other useful books, please contact me at markey@MRgrp-us.com, visit my website at MRgrp-us.com, or call me at 802 373 7789.

Be Fabulous & Prosper,

Markey Read

Acknowledgements

I am deeply grateful to my clients who have bravely donned their entrepreneurial capes and launched so many amazing businesses. It was with you that I developed and tested my ideas as we explored, designed, and built your enterprises. I am grateful for all of you who trusted me on your path. I learned as much or more from you as you did from me.

I am indebted to the Women's Small Business Program (WSBP) and New England Culinary Institute (NECI) for inviting me to be on their multi-disciplinary teaching teams in the 2000s. Joining the WSBP team to teach *Start up* helped me develop a more fully rounded view of how to build a business. And subsequently joining the Business Management faculty at NECI allowed me to simultaneously expand my culinary knowledge and apply my business acumen in a completely unique environment.

Along the way, there have been numerous mentors, teachers, partners, coaches, and colleagues who held the light when the path was foggy and joyously celebrated my many accomplishments. Three people were especially pivotal. Tim King, my husband, business partner and dear friend of 30+ years, who regularly reminds me of who I am and calls me forward to be even more. Toni Stone, coach, mentor, and friend who for 25 years encouraged me to wear my entrepreneurial cape with pride as I forged fresh territory as a coach, teacher, and mentor while learning how to be a business partner with my husband. My mother, Grace Hart, who has been creating and selling her art since before I was even conceived; she ignited my enterprising interest when she taught me to sell puppets at the Renaissance Pleasure Faire in Southern California in the early 1960s.

The spark for this book came in 2015, shortly after I published my last book, Leadership Styles. Since I had left WSBP and NECI, I no longer had a formal platform from which to teach entrepreneurialism and I was seeking books and materials to use with clients. I took bits from one resource and bobs from another and handed clients a Frankenstein-ish collection of materials. I am grateful to all the people who have written books and created materials that I could access and share with my clients.

Initially, the task was to write a comprehensive guide for entrepreneurs, but this proved to be too much. When I let go of writing the guide for entrepreneurs to end all guides and started writing what I know, however, this book is what resulted.

Turns out, I know a lot about being in business because I have been at it for nearly all of my life. As a teenager, I made and sold things to my friends; as a new graduate freelancer, I hawked articles to various publications; as a young woman, I made and sold custom clothing to women. In my mid -20s, I researched and published *Vermont's Most Complete Book of Bed & Breakfasts* and personally peddled it to stores throughout Vermont, and finally in my late-20's I was given an opportunity to join a consulting company as a partner because I was really good at enrolling clients and closing deals. That was in 1992 and I never looked back.

I am grateful to the people who waited patiently for me to count their change at the Faire, my high school friends who funded my pocket money, the editors and publishers who accepted my articles, the women who hired me to make them clothing, the bed and breakfast owners who agreed to be listed in my book, the store owners who displayed my book, and to Tim King for seeing that we could be a dynamic duo as we supported each other as entrepreneurs who dove deeply into our interests to create high value for our clients. Without all of you and the lessons you taught me along the way, I would be a lesser person and this book would not be the same.

And you, my dear reader, I am eternally grateful that you have picked up this book and used it to forward your entrepreneurial journey. May you continue to grow and prosper as a Solopreneur!